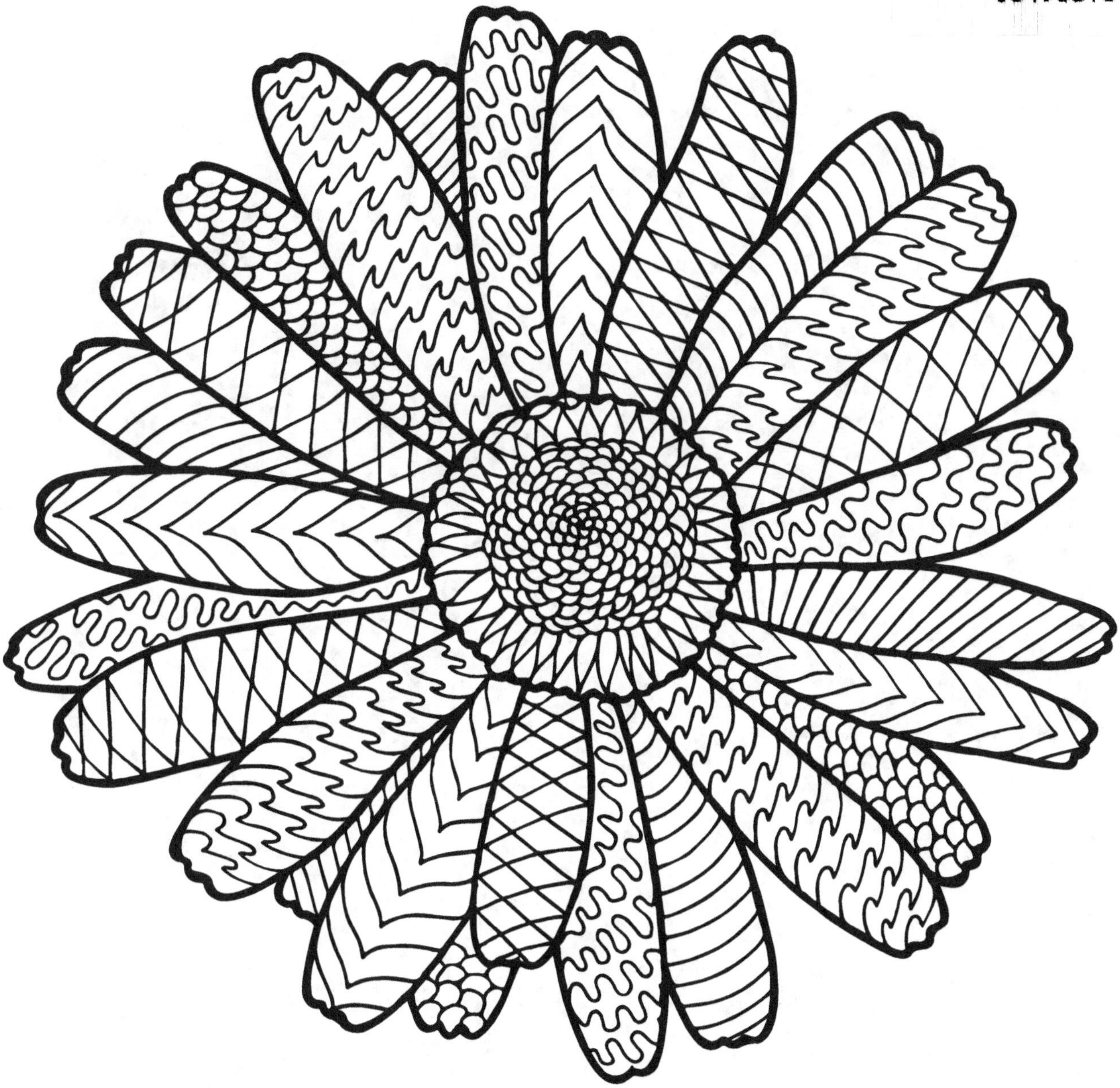

Copyright 2020 by Devyn Brewer

Please do not reproduce, scan, or distribute any part of this book in any form without permission of the author.

ISBN 9798621987664
Independently published

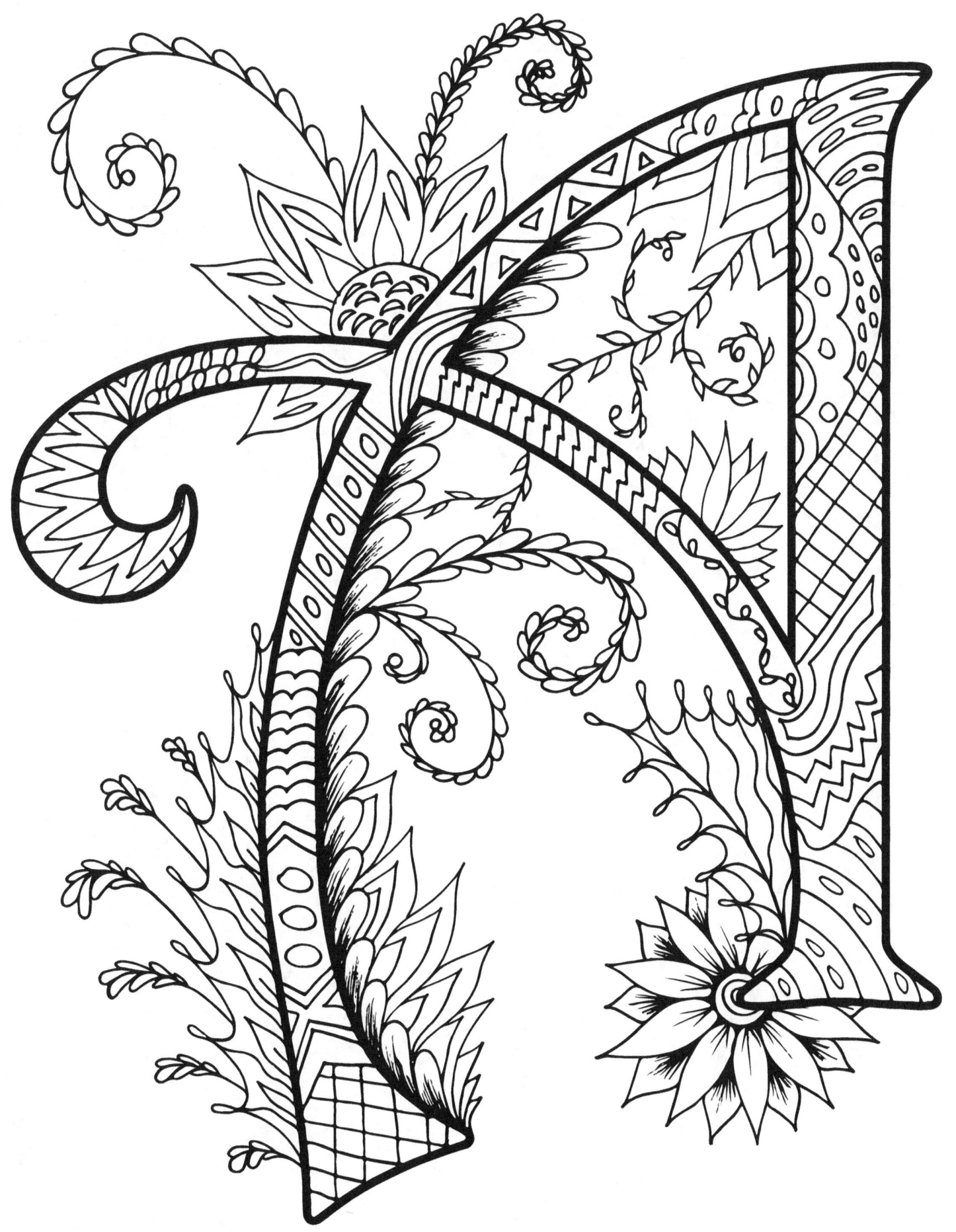

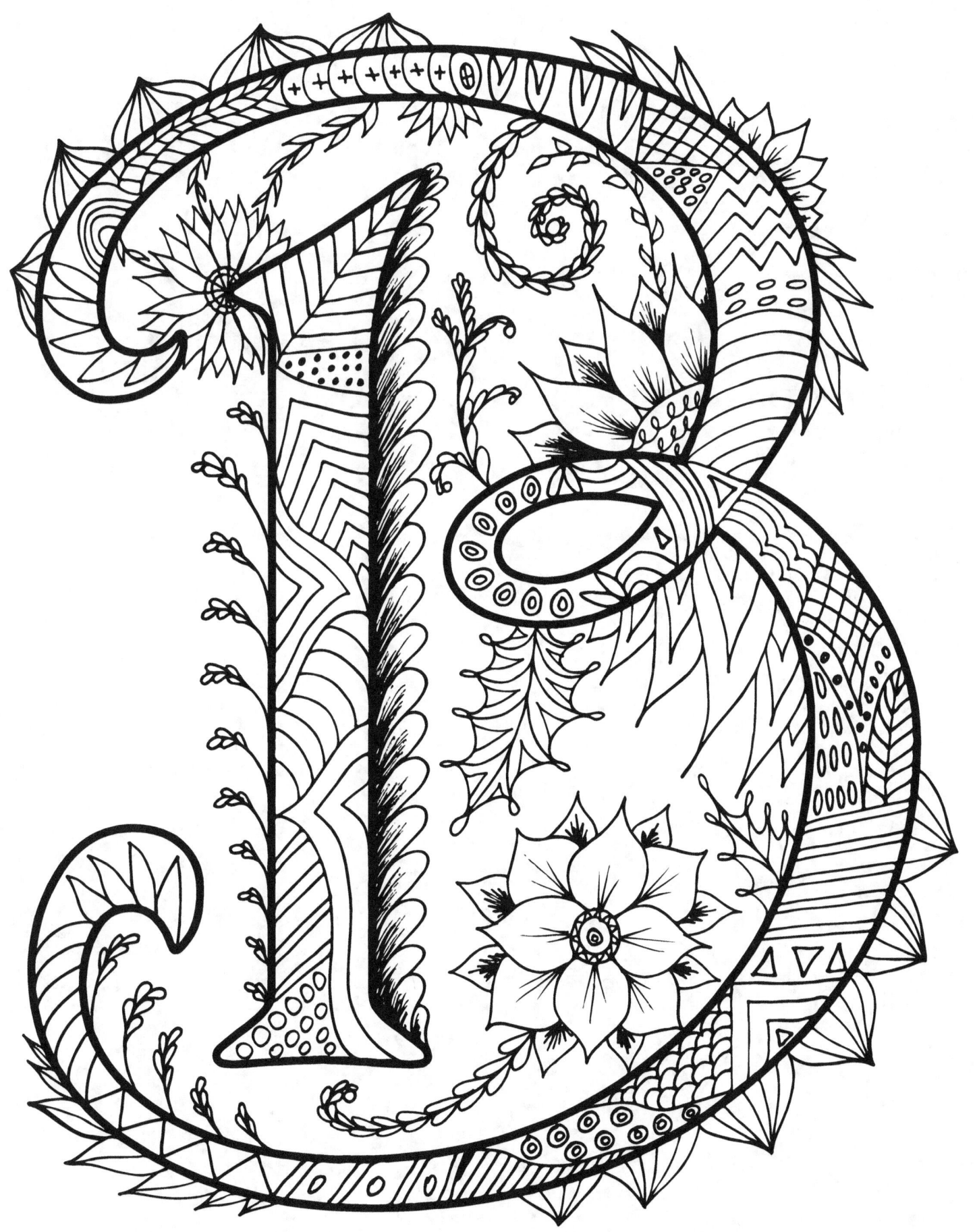

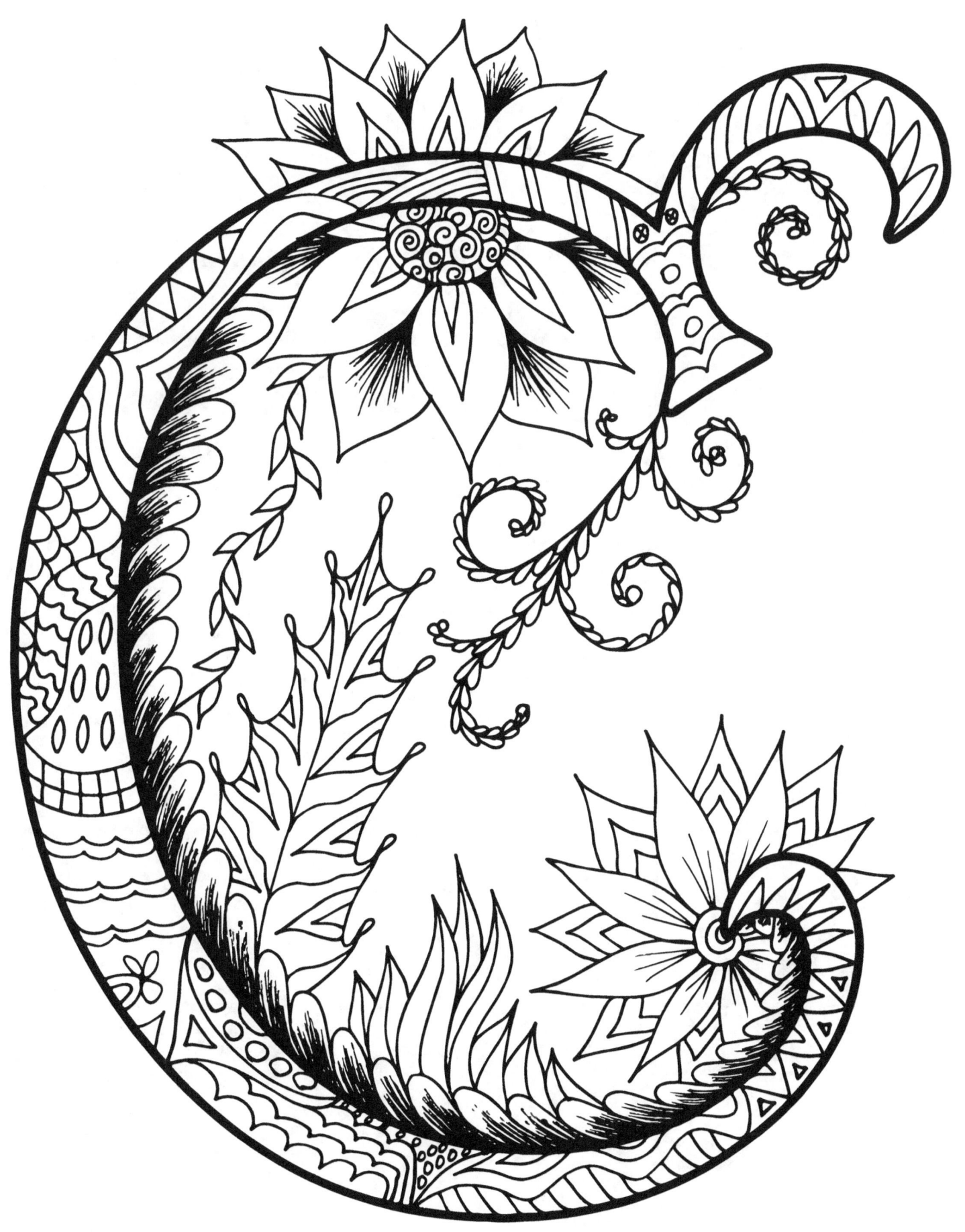

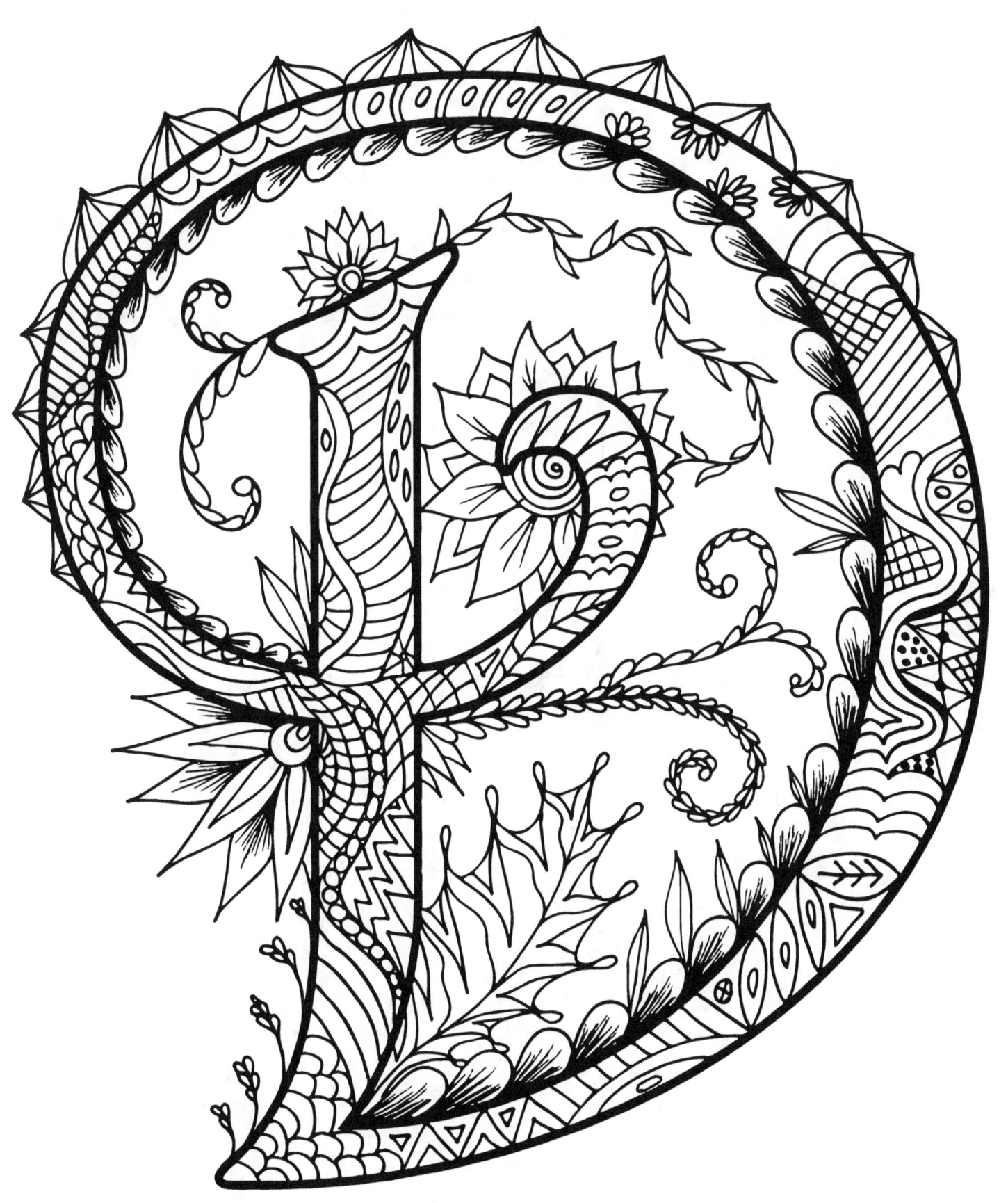

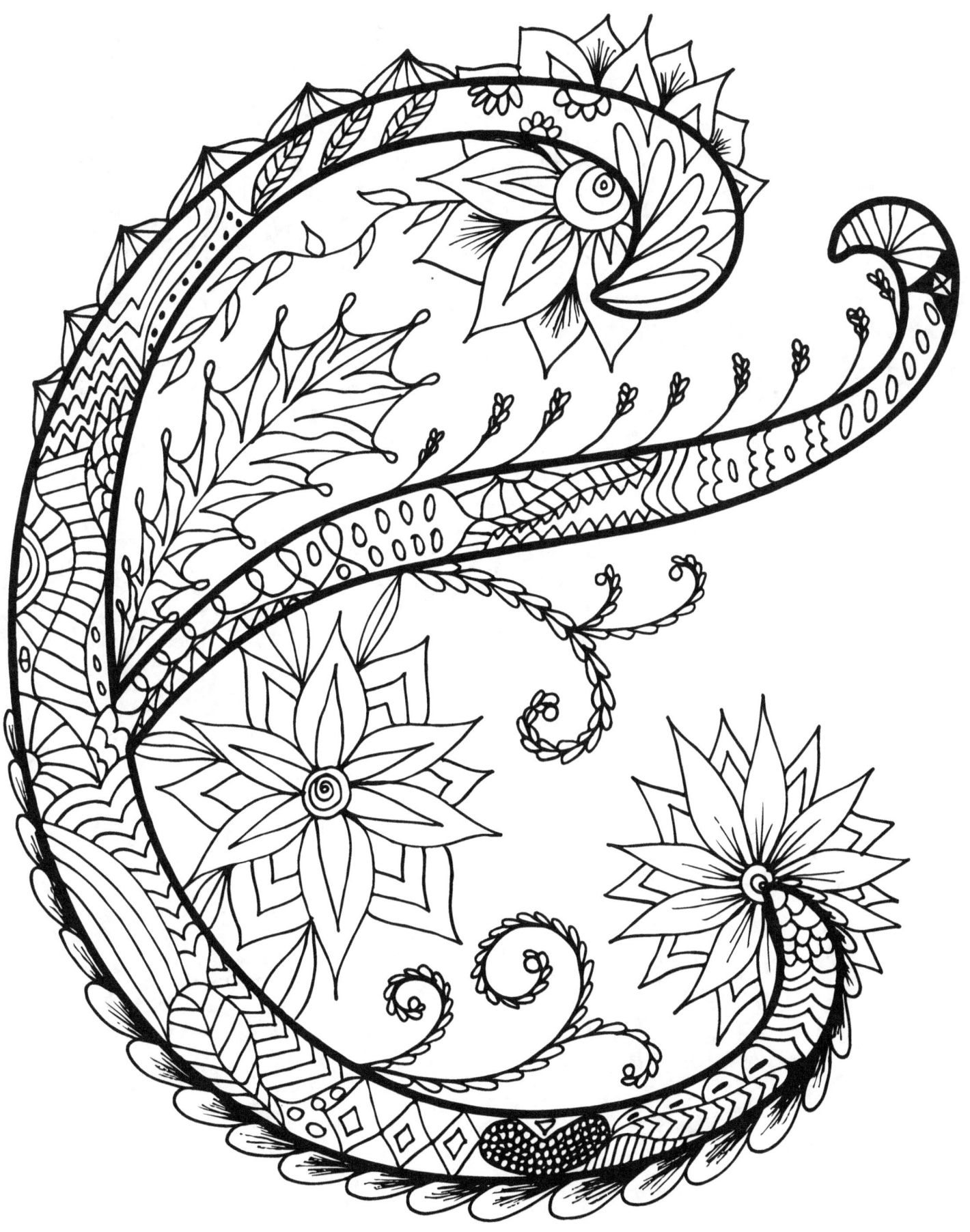

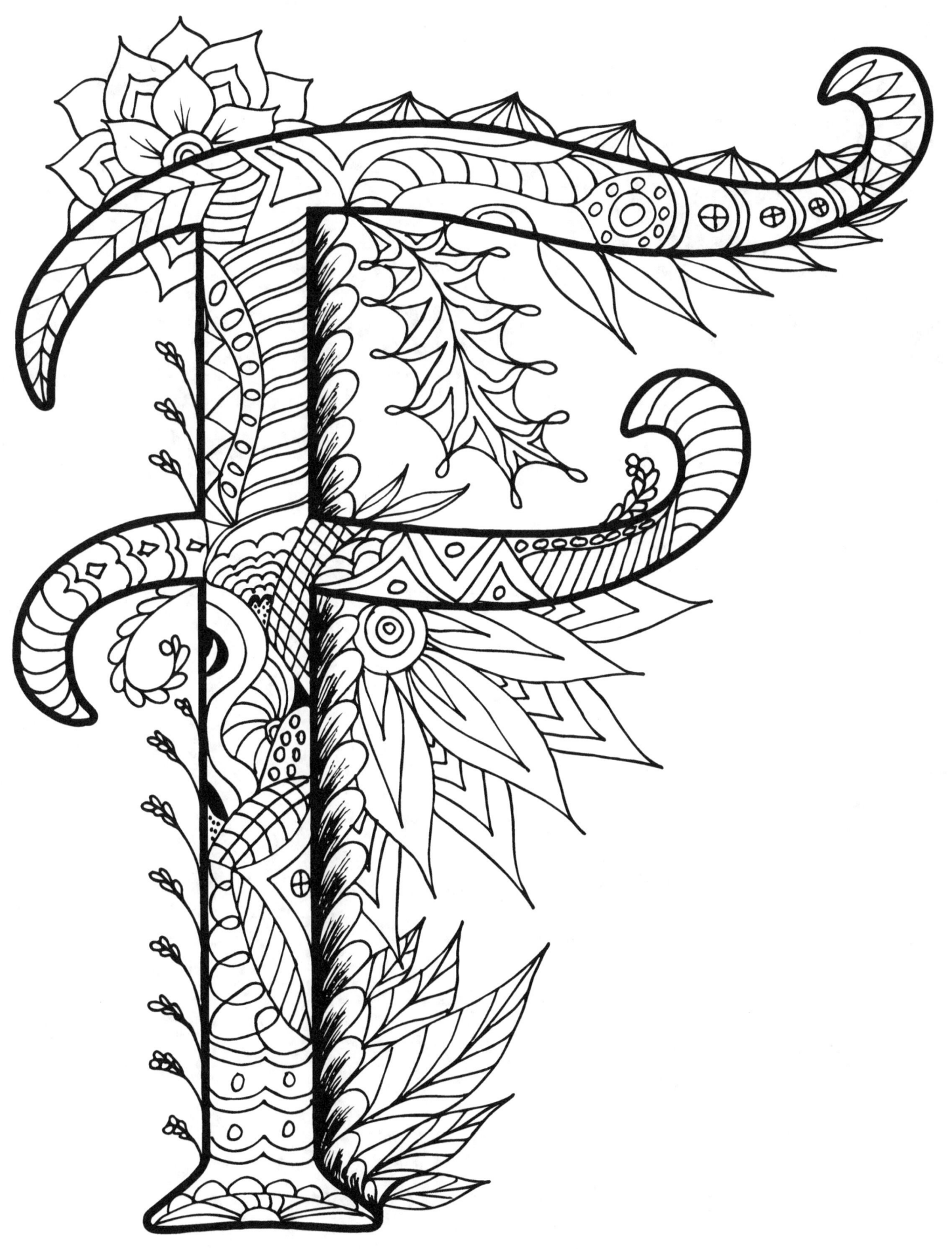

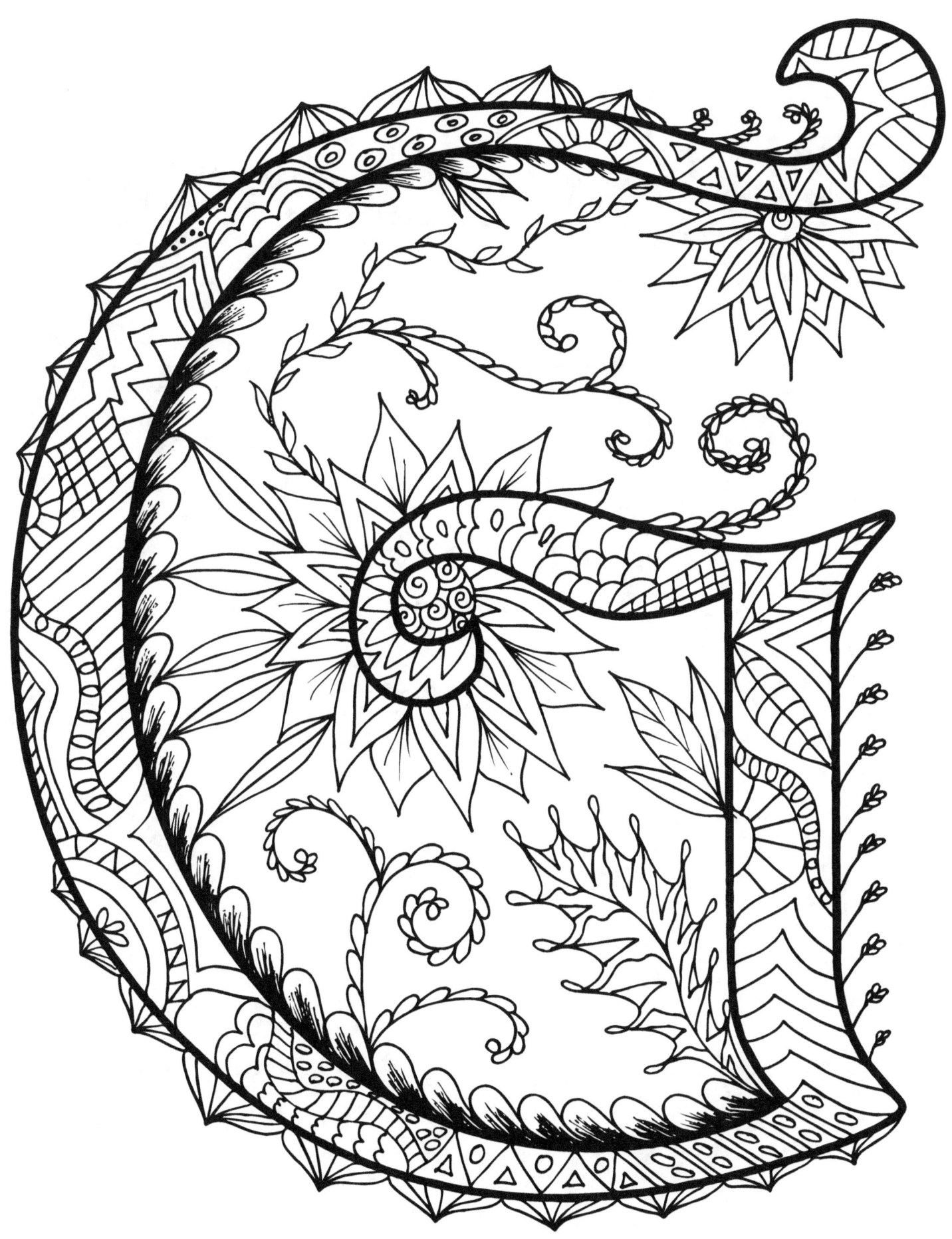

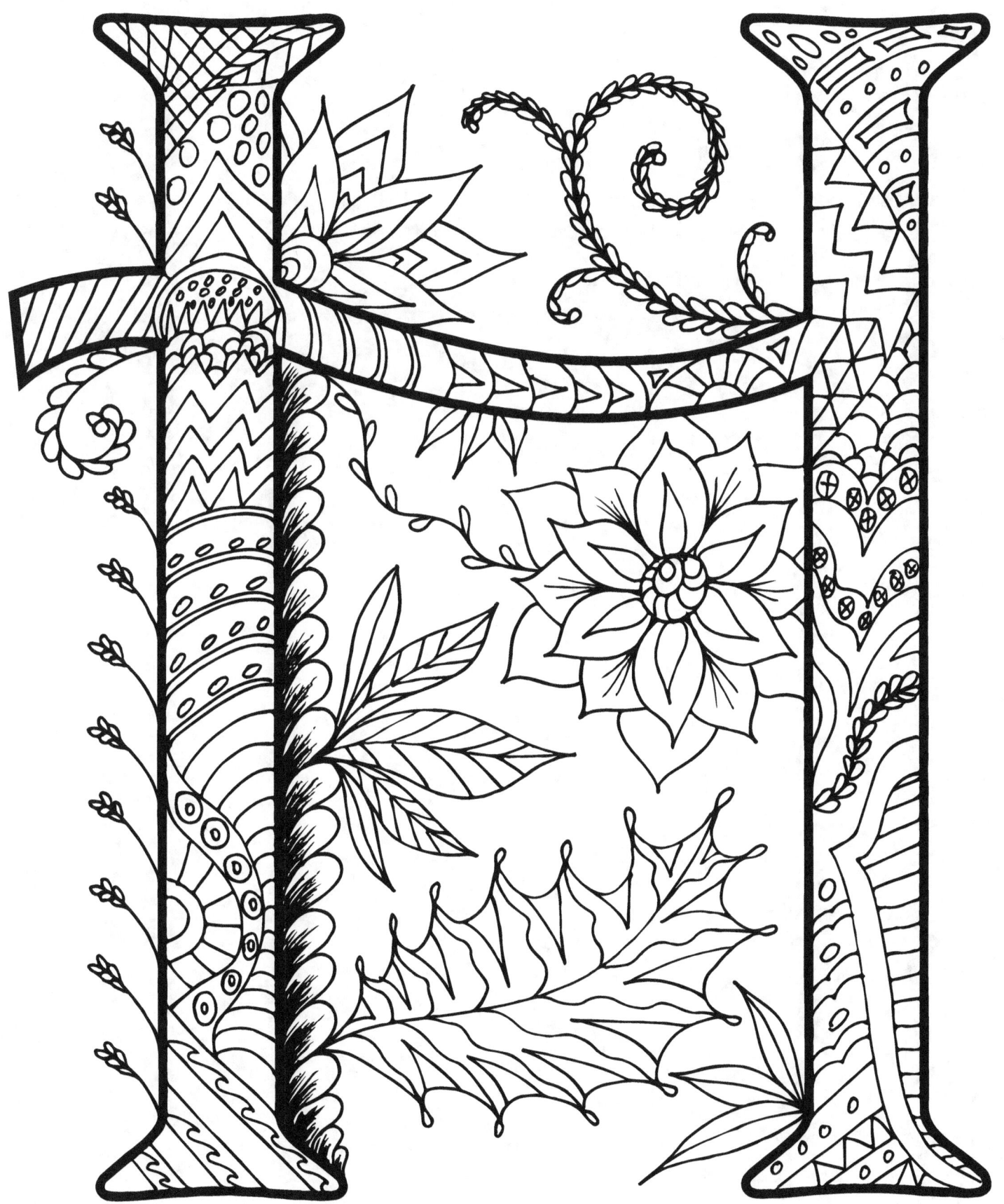

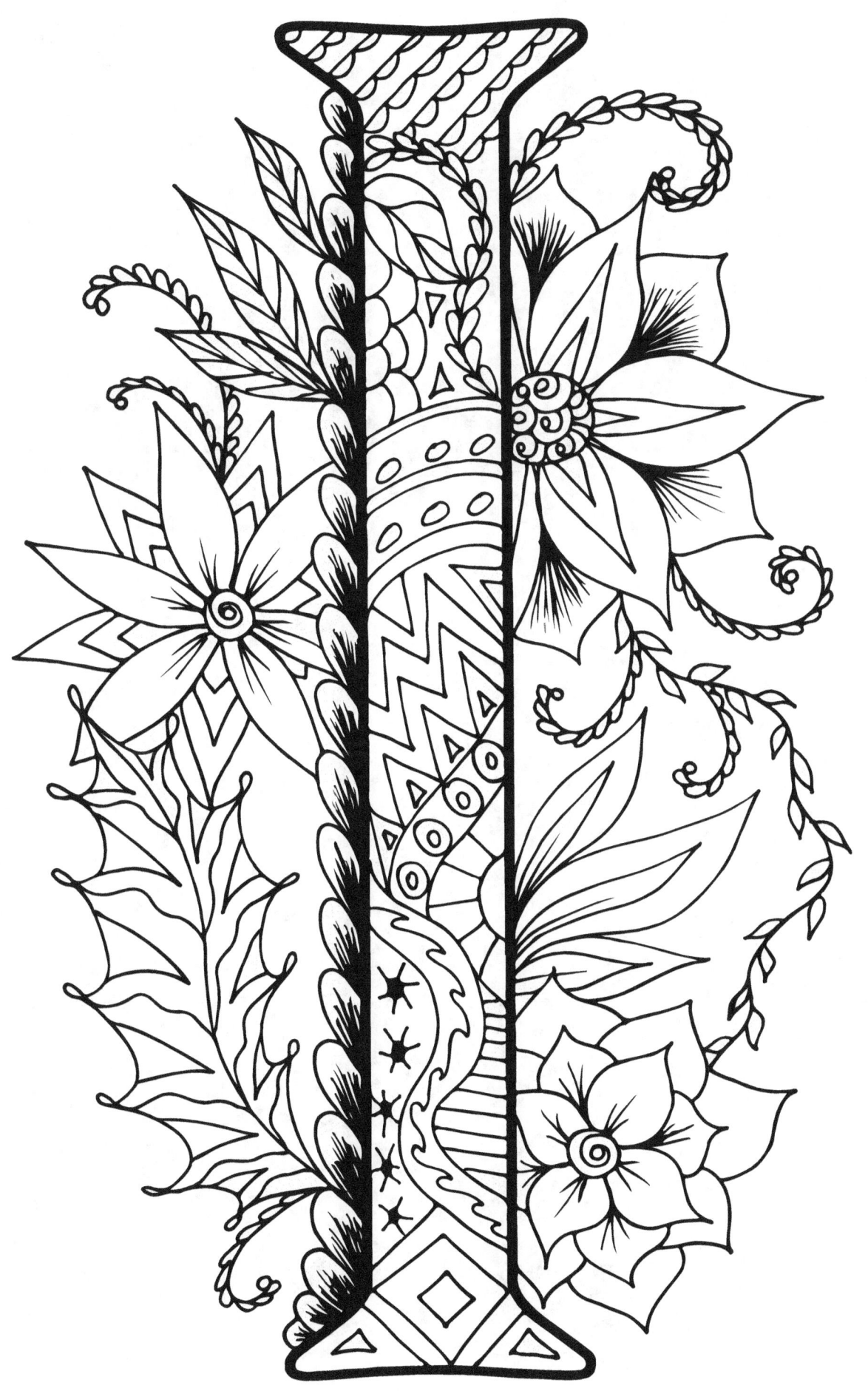

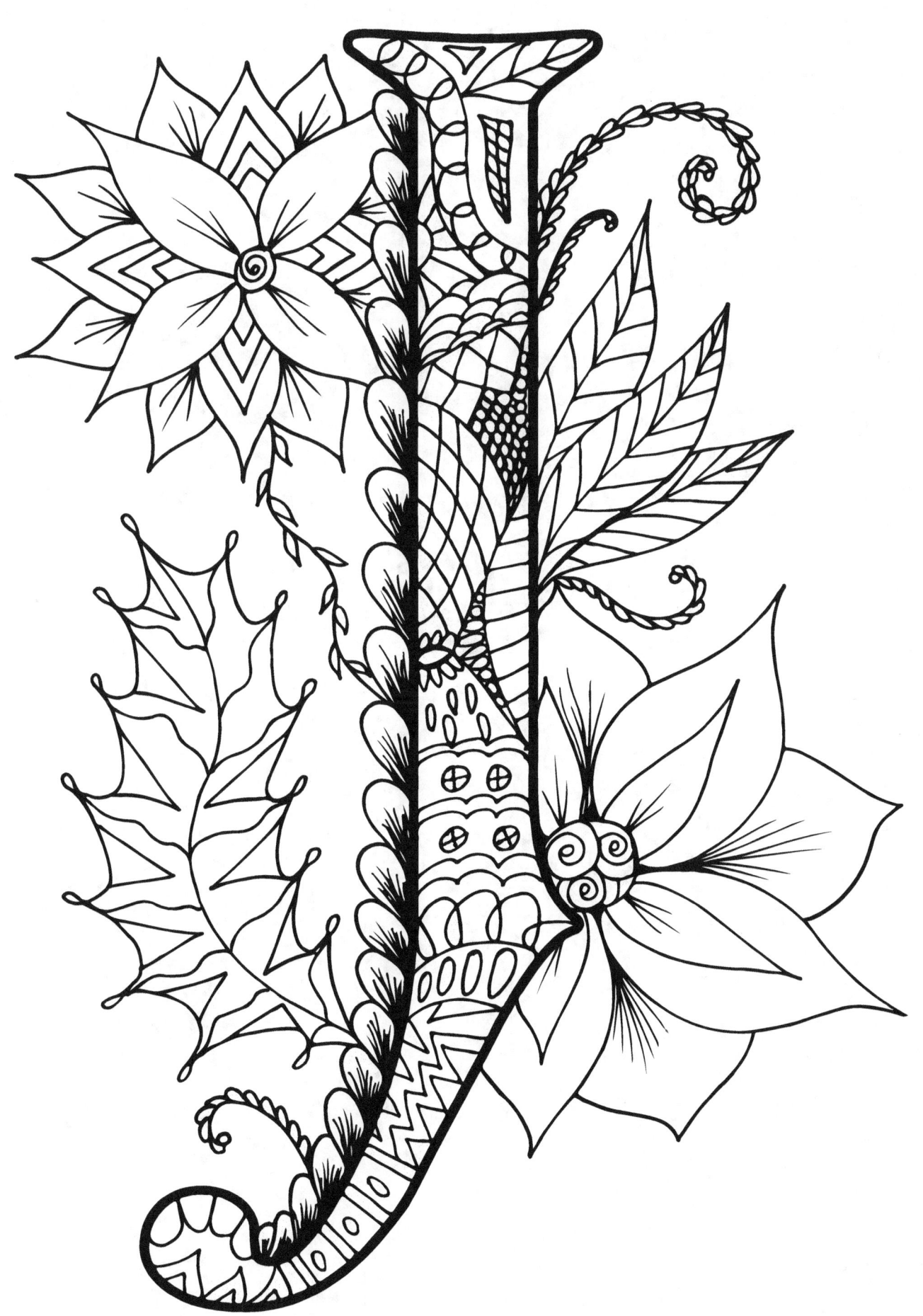

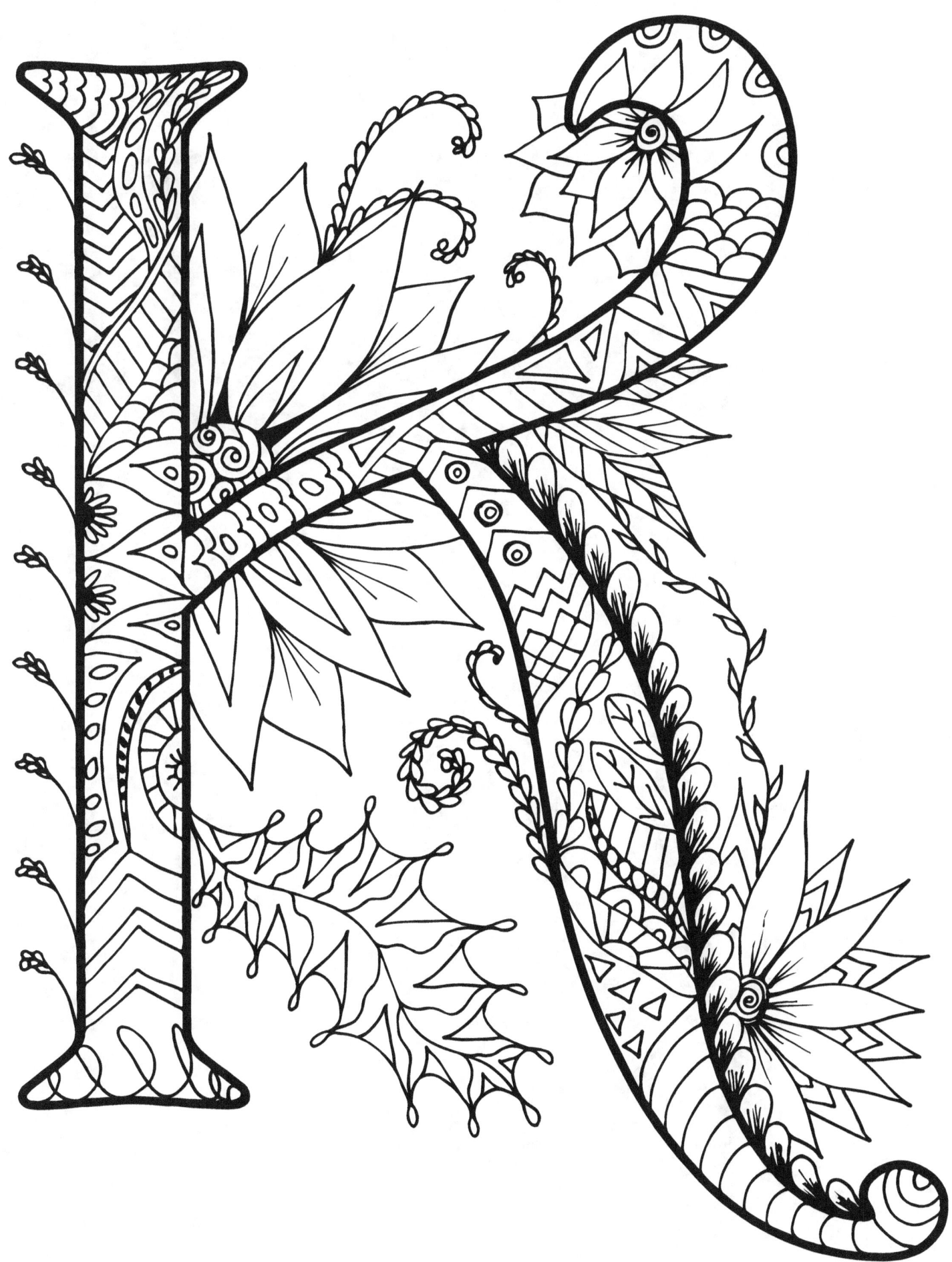

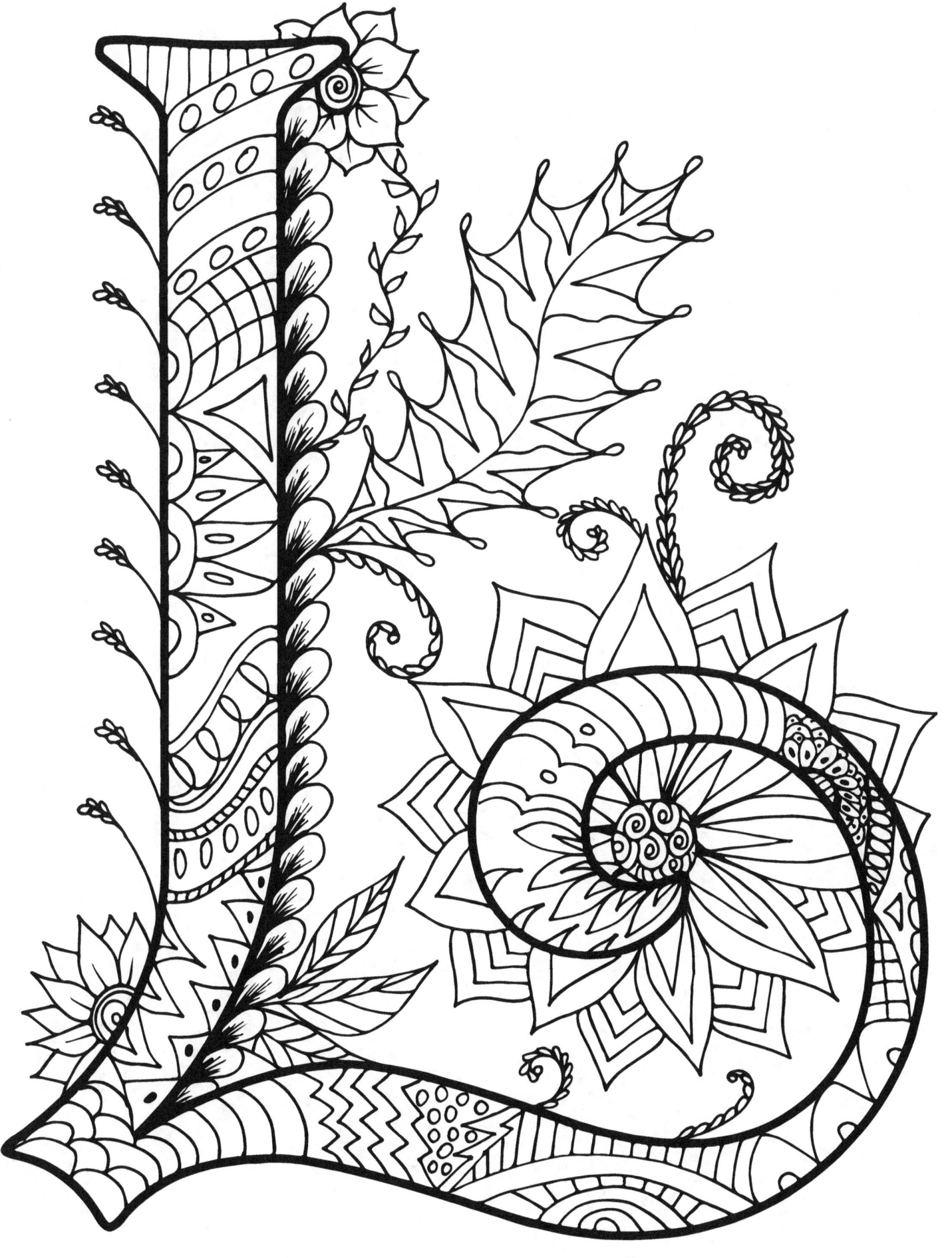

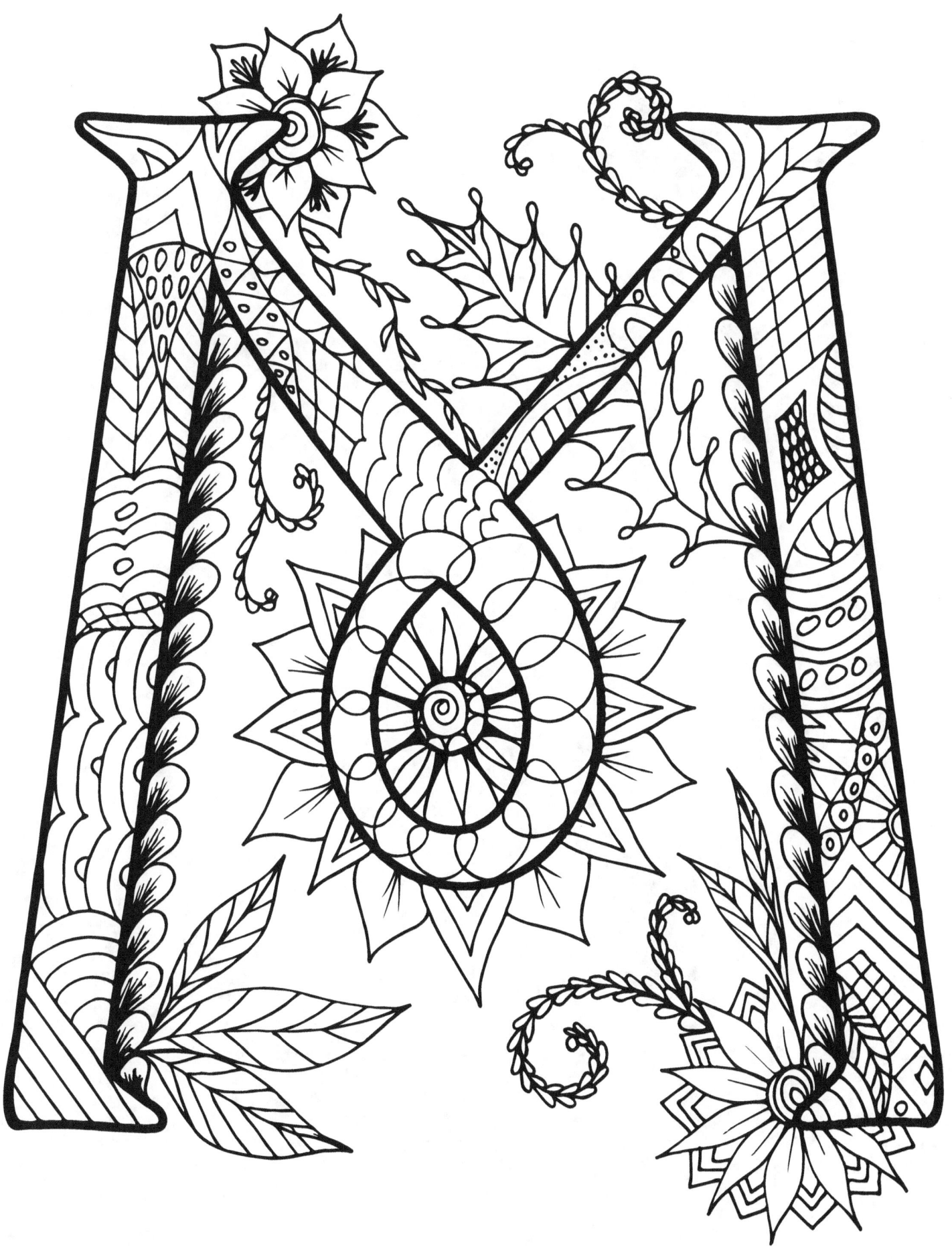

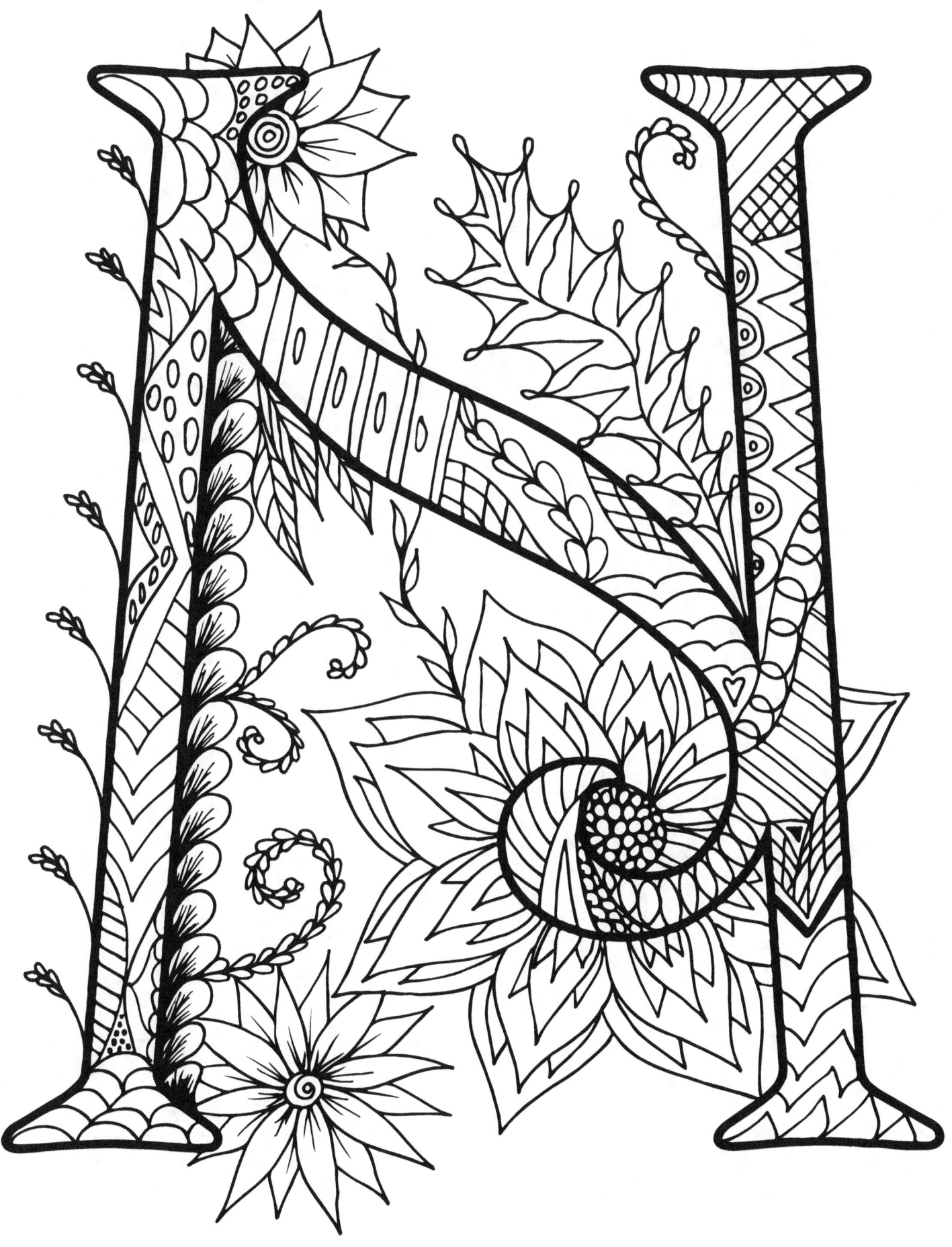

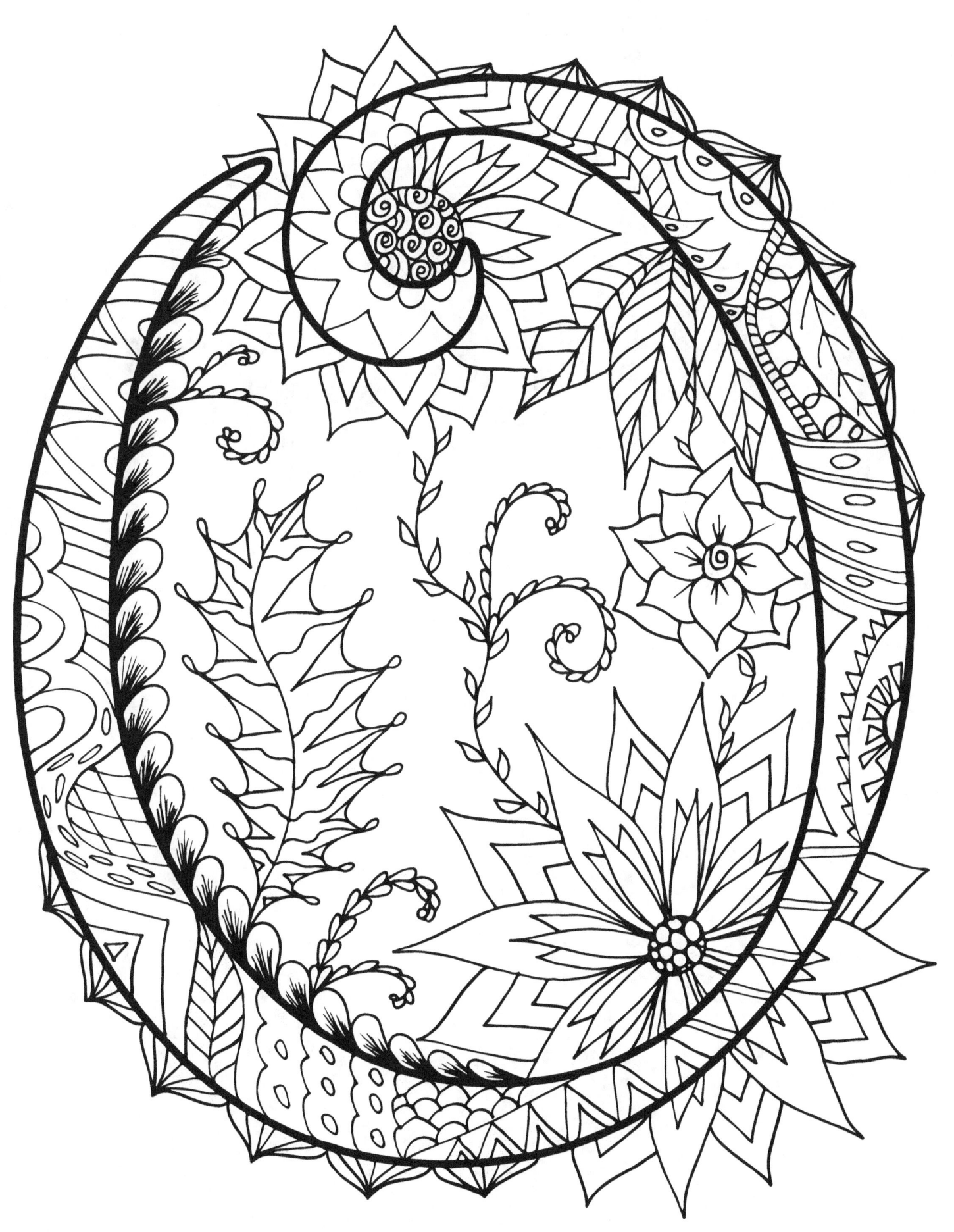

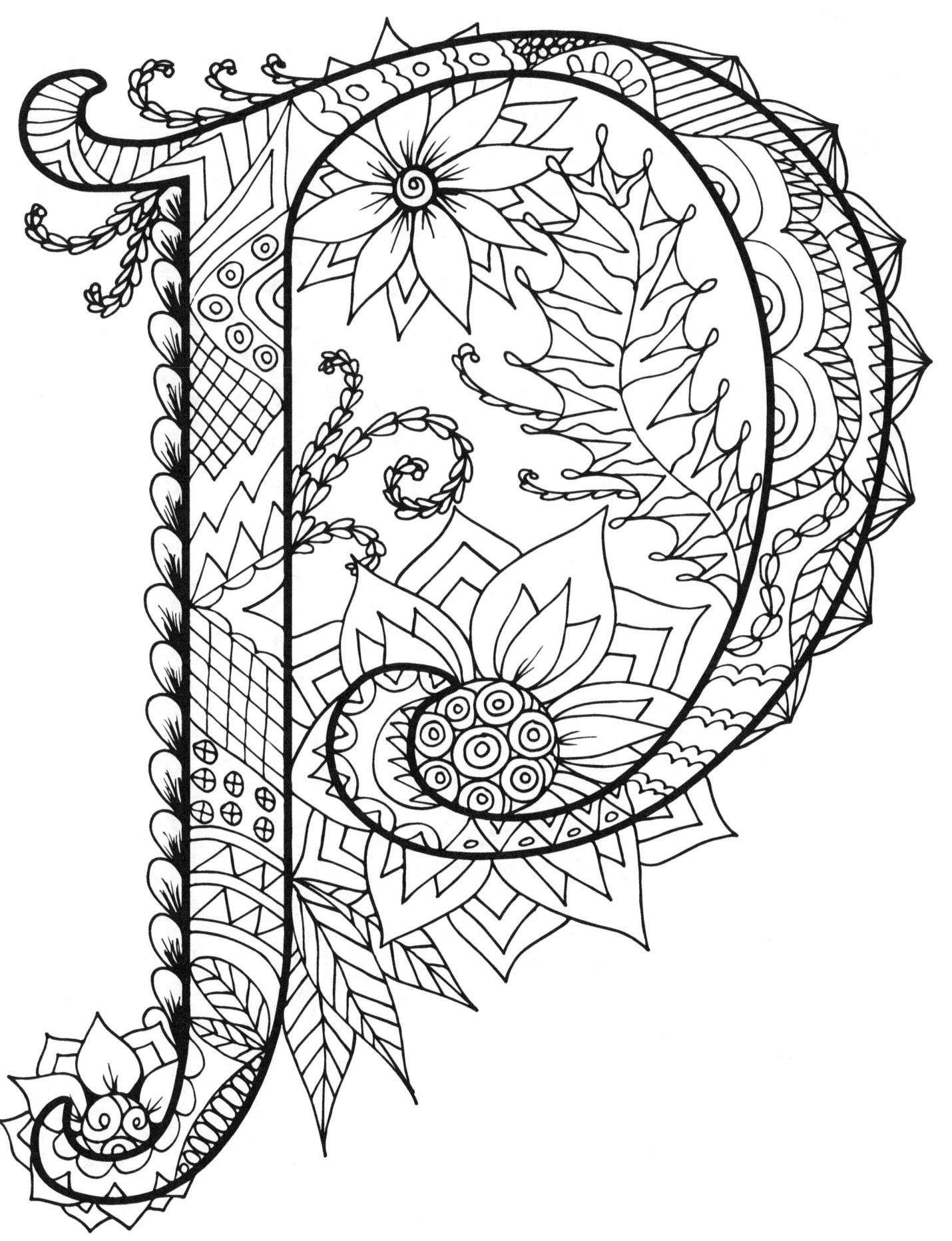

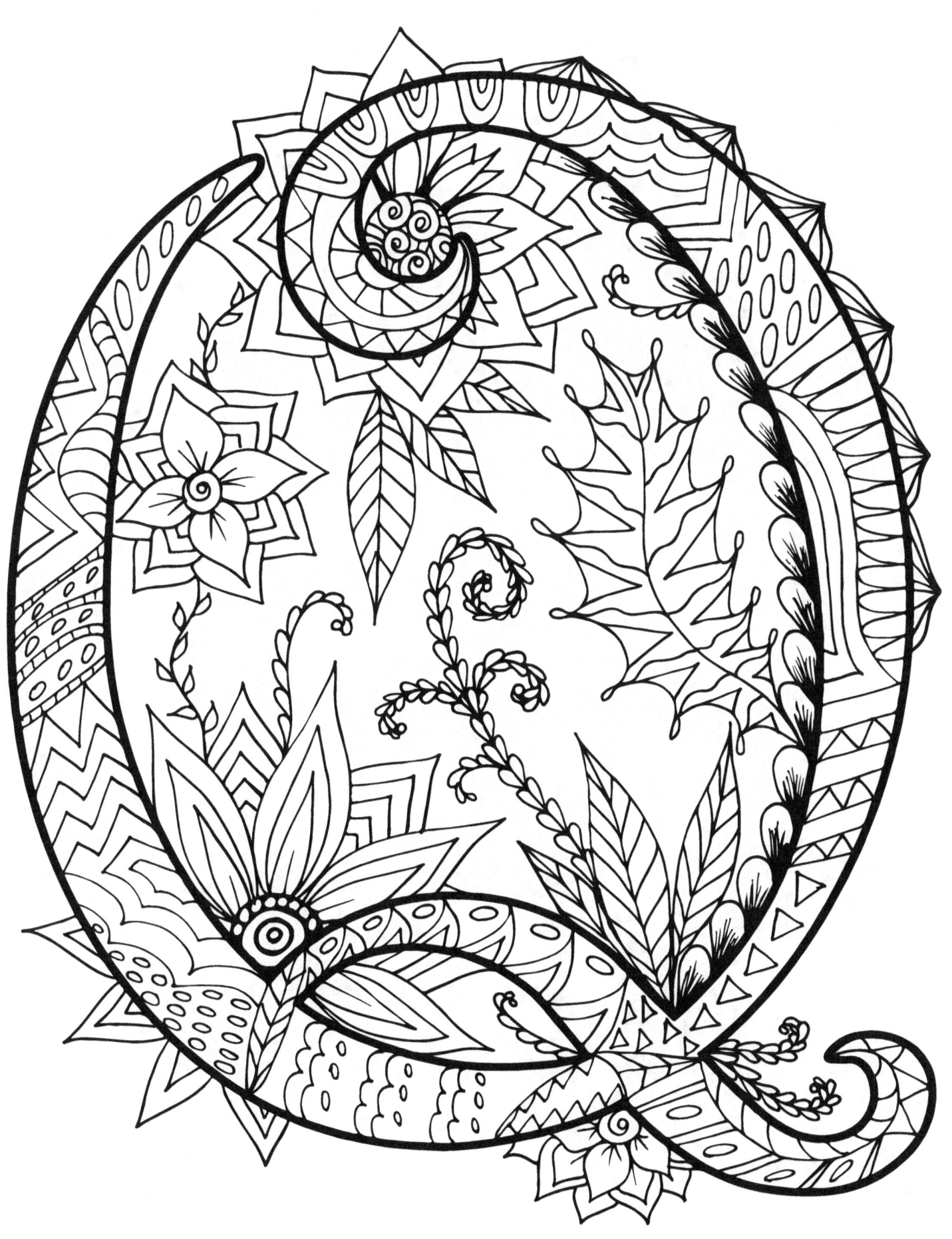

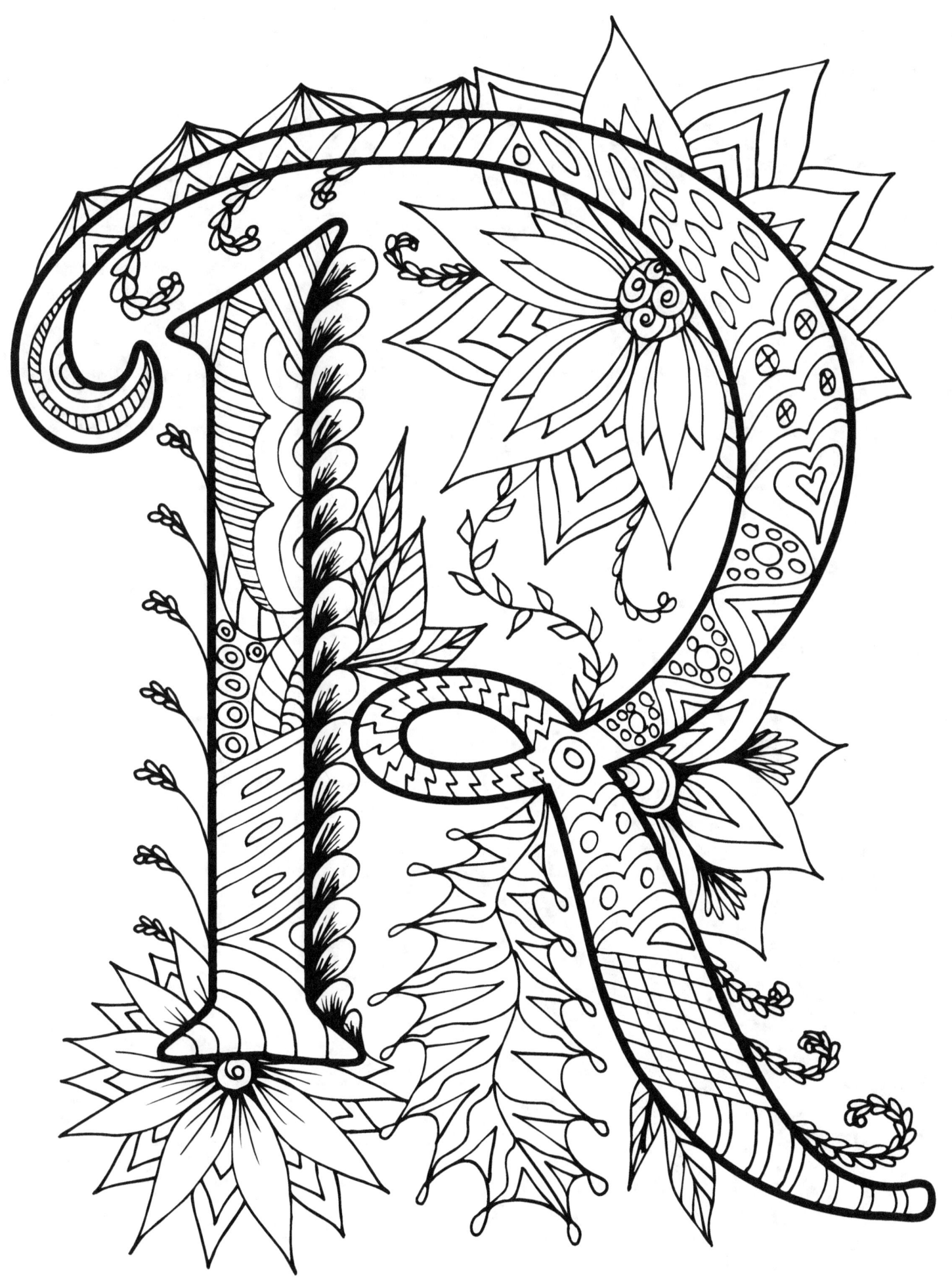

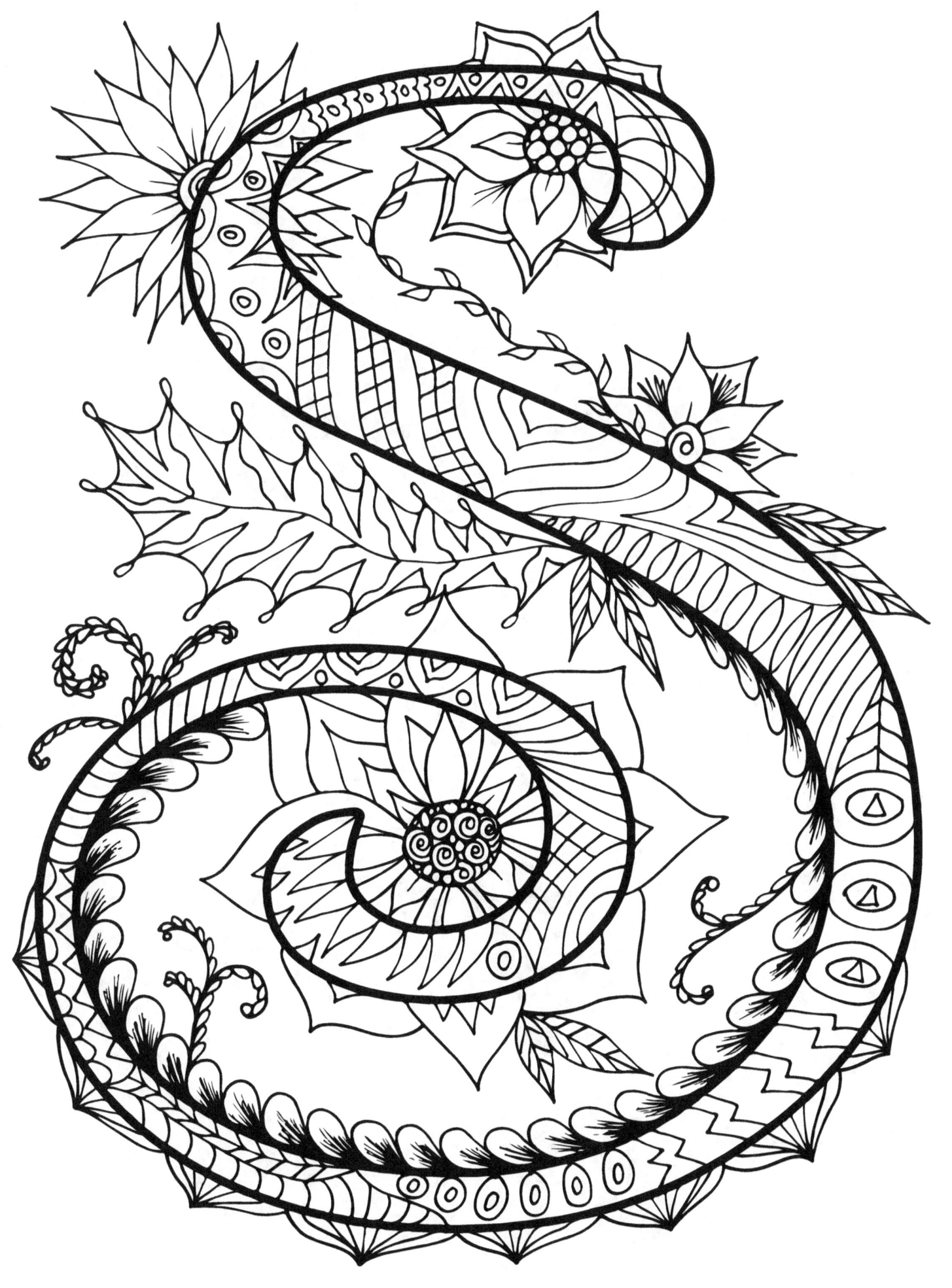

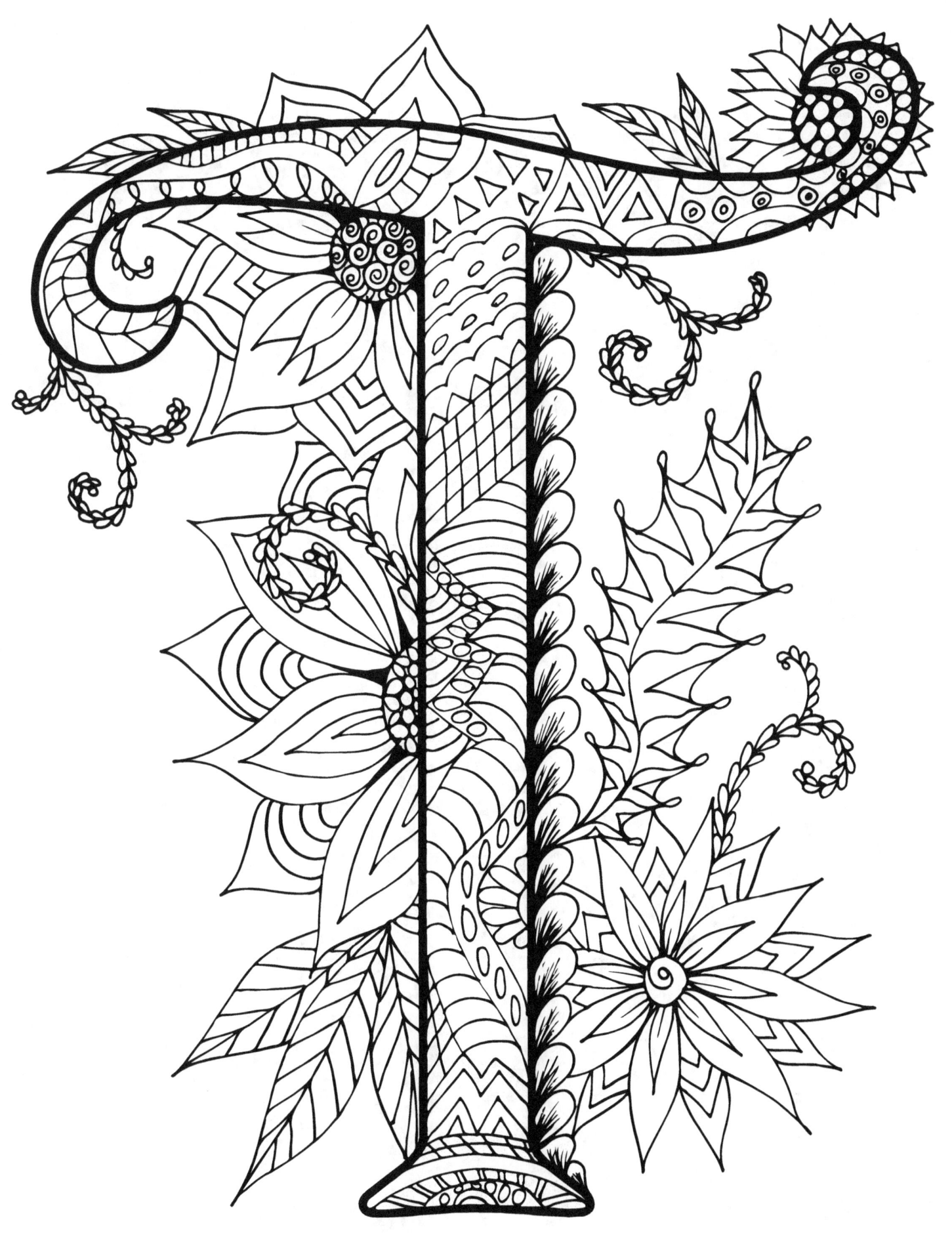

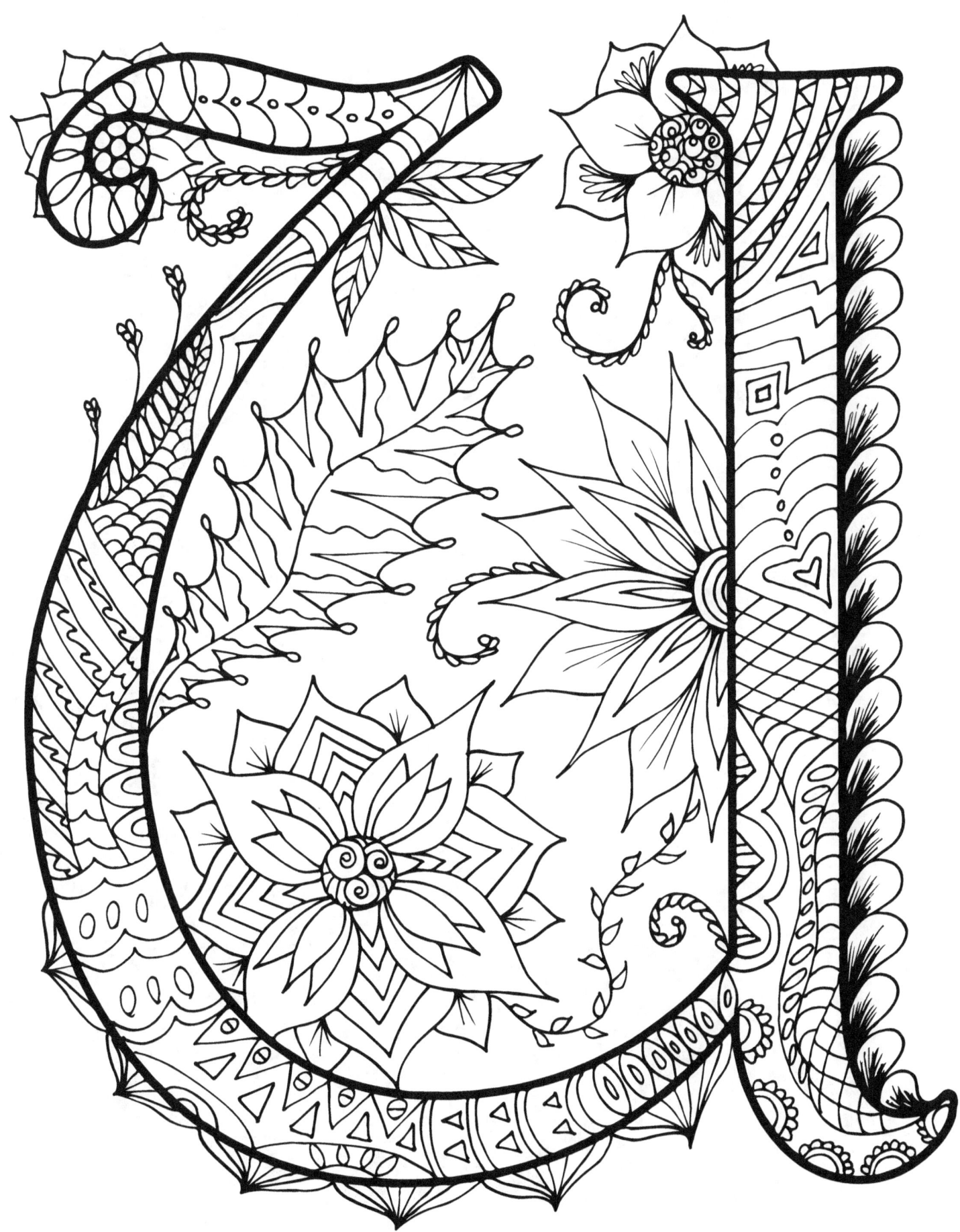

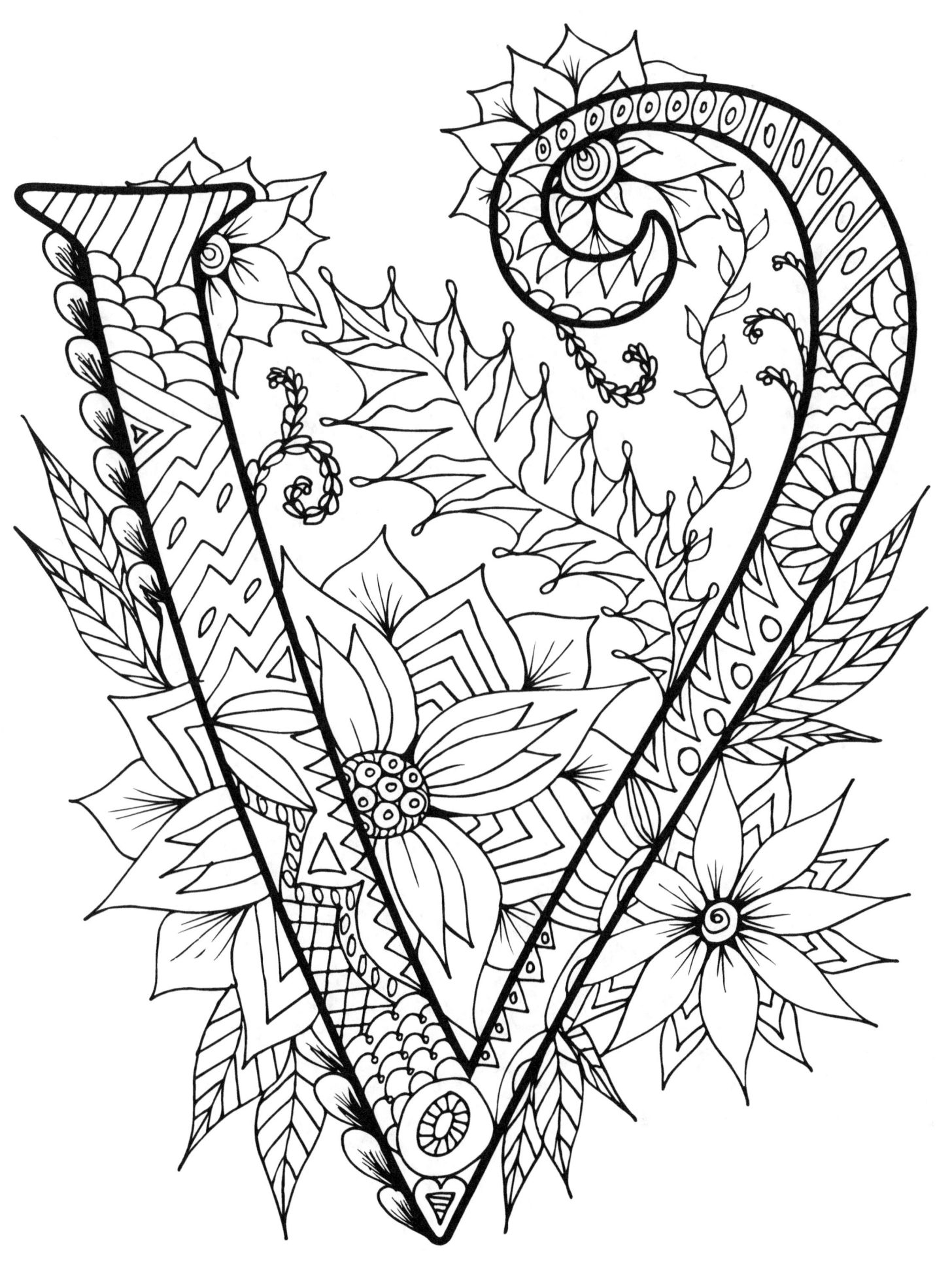

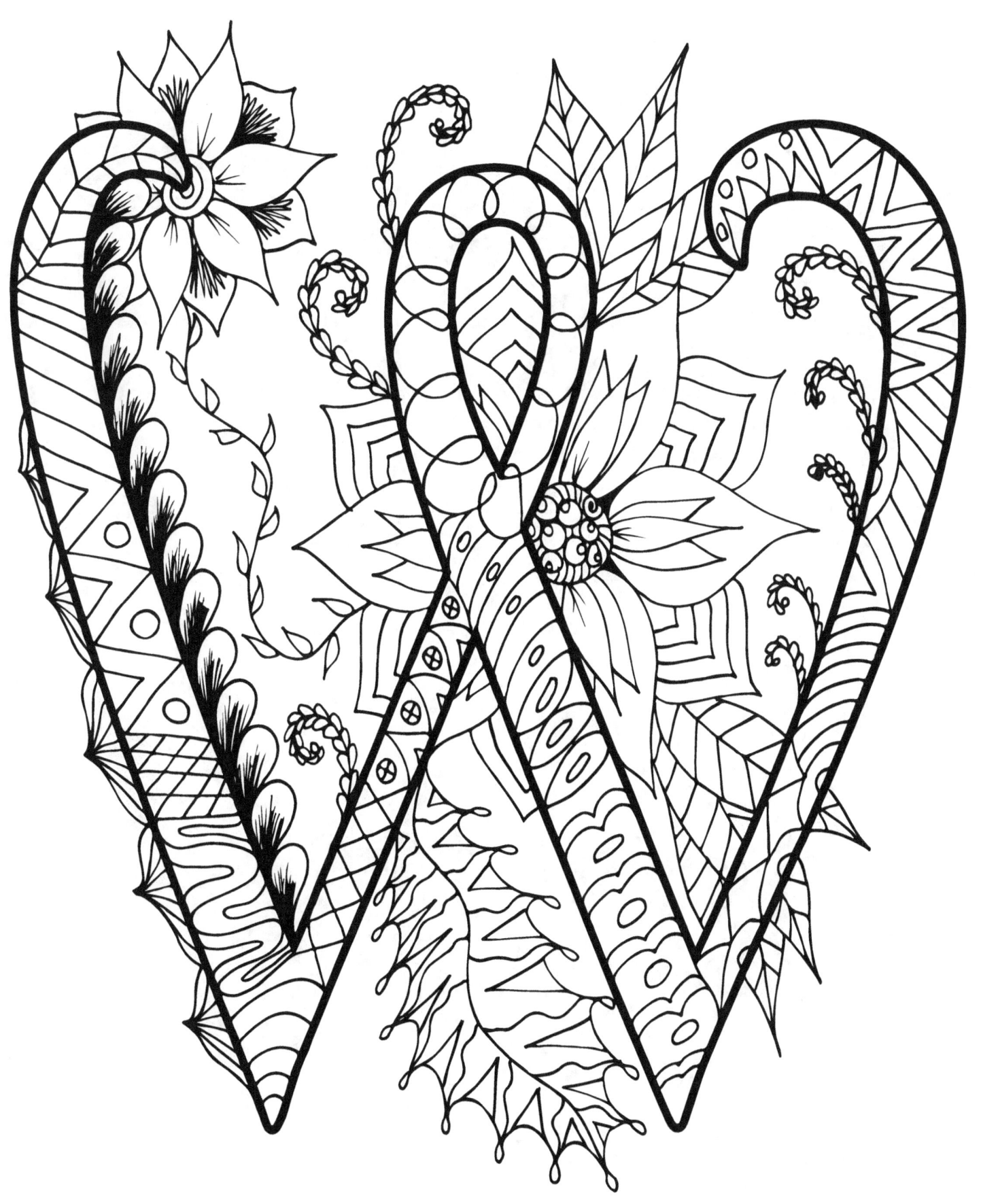

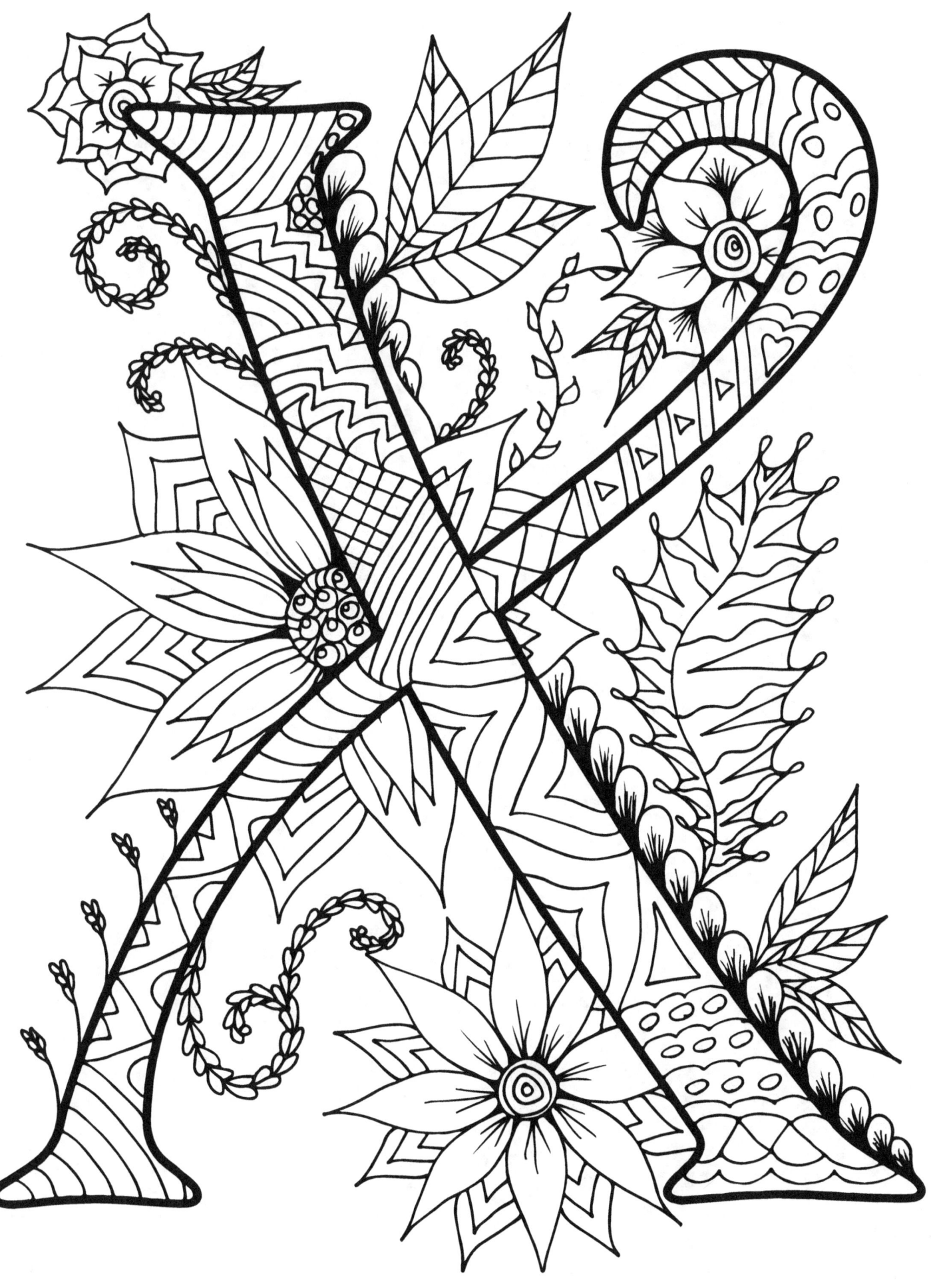

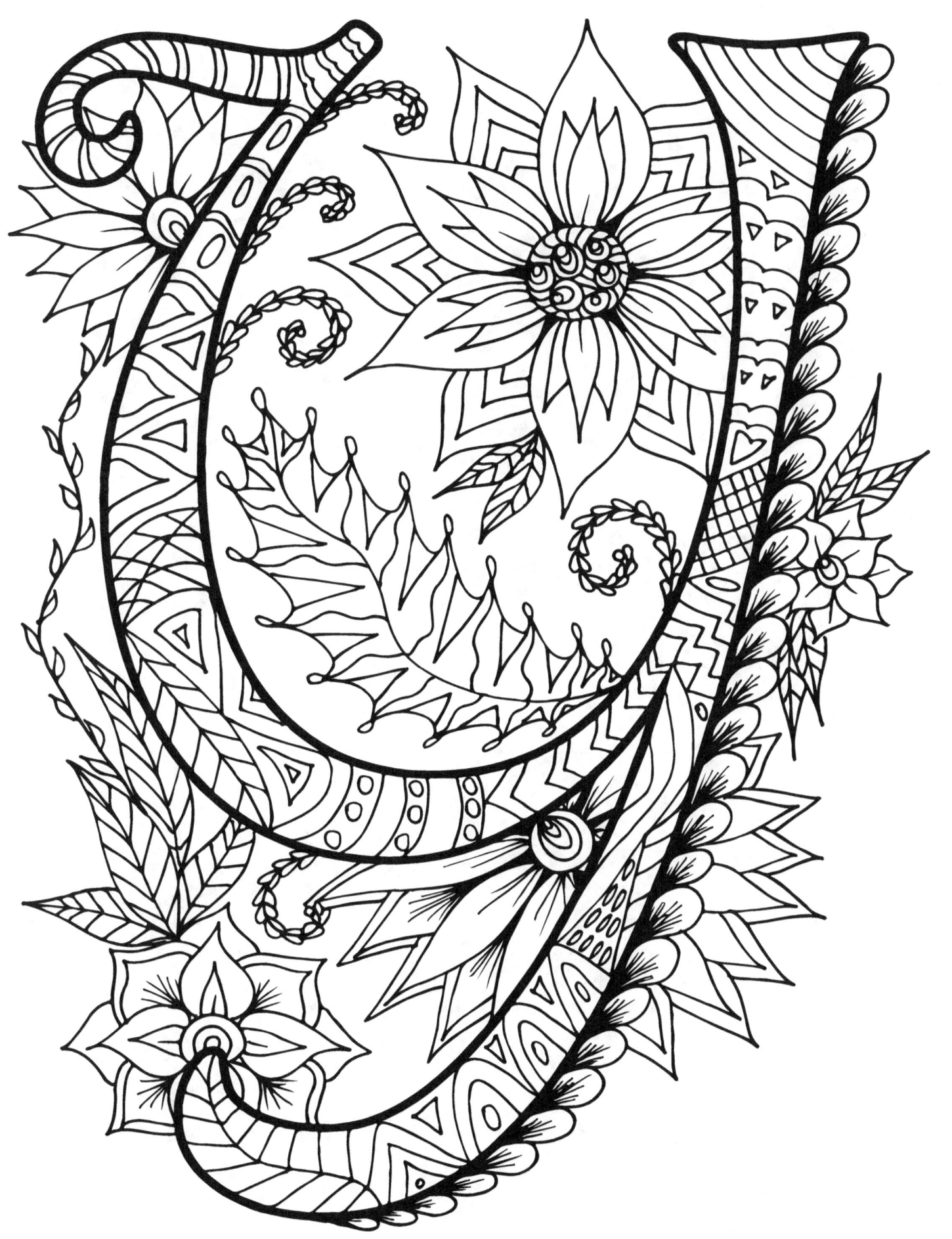

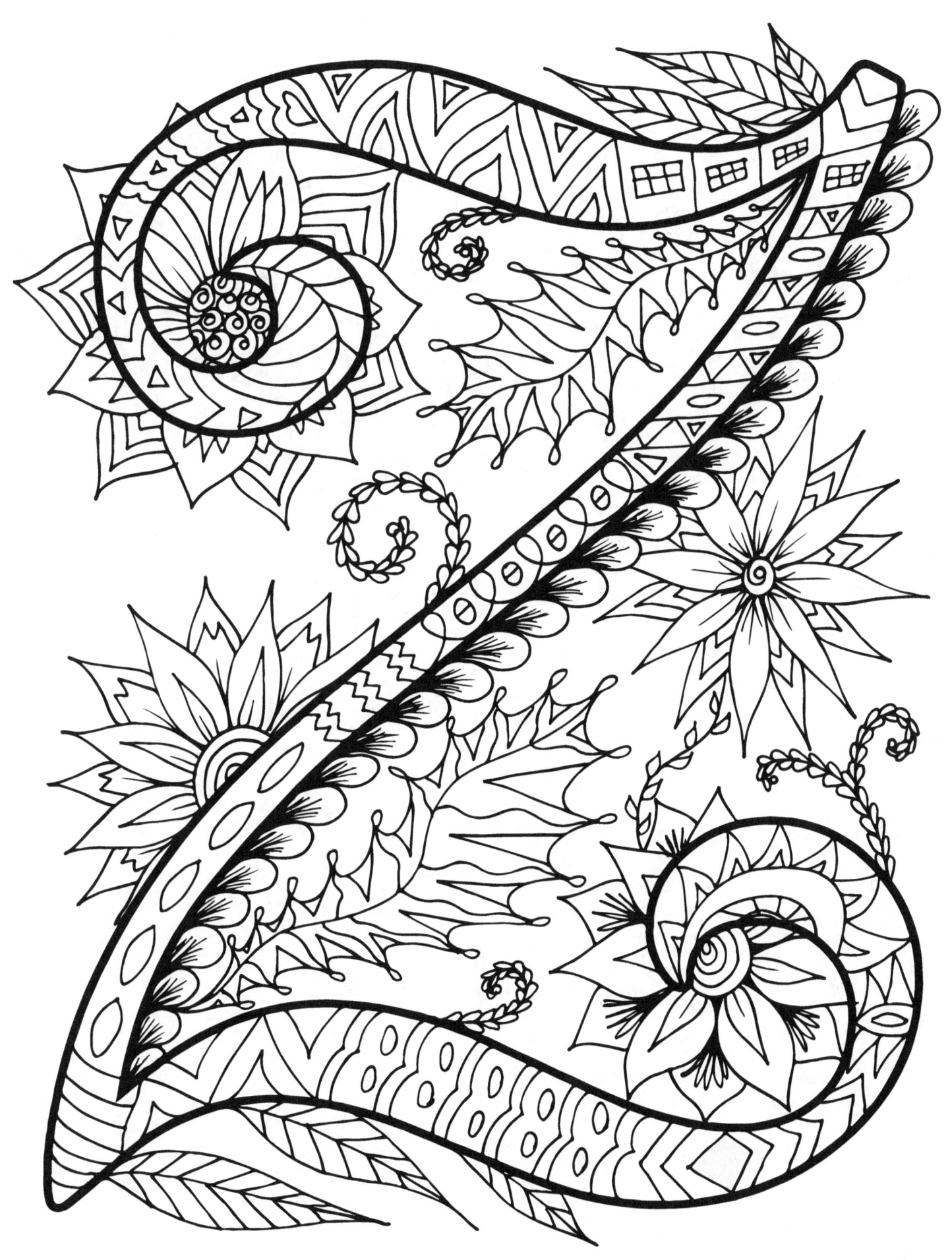

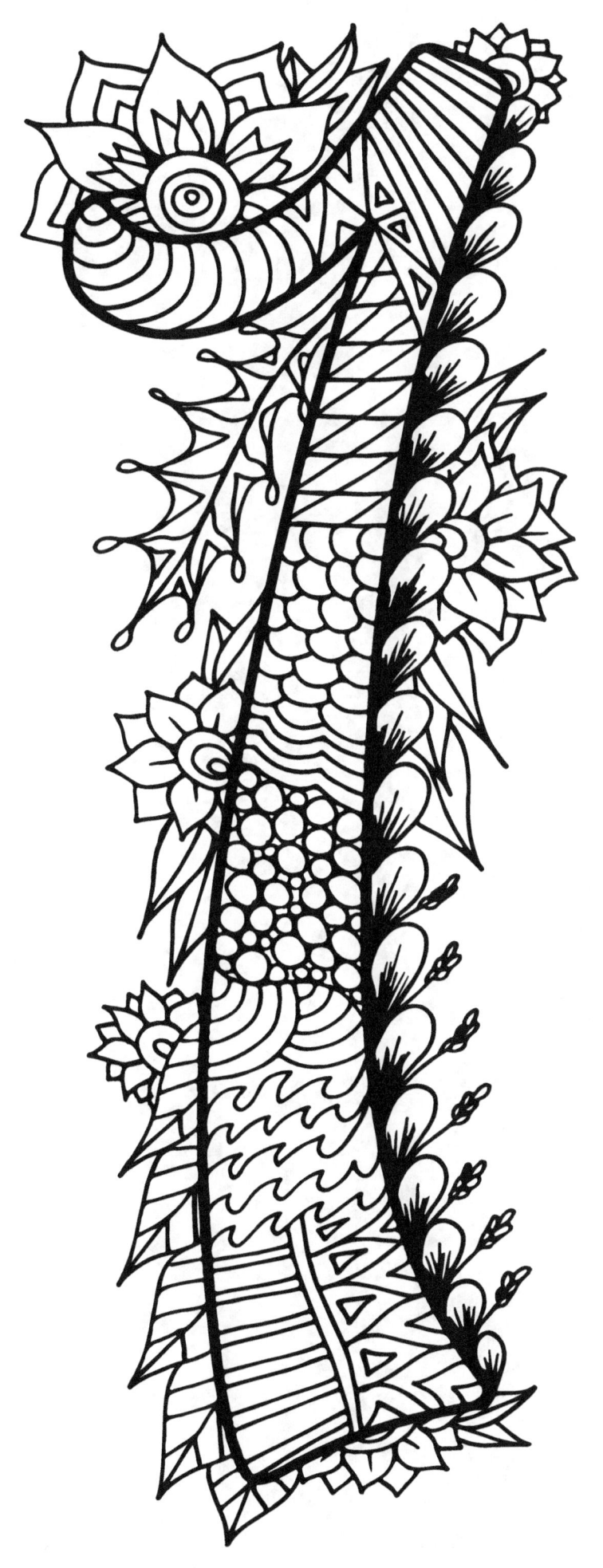

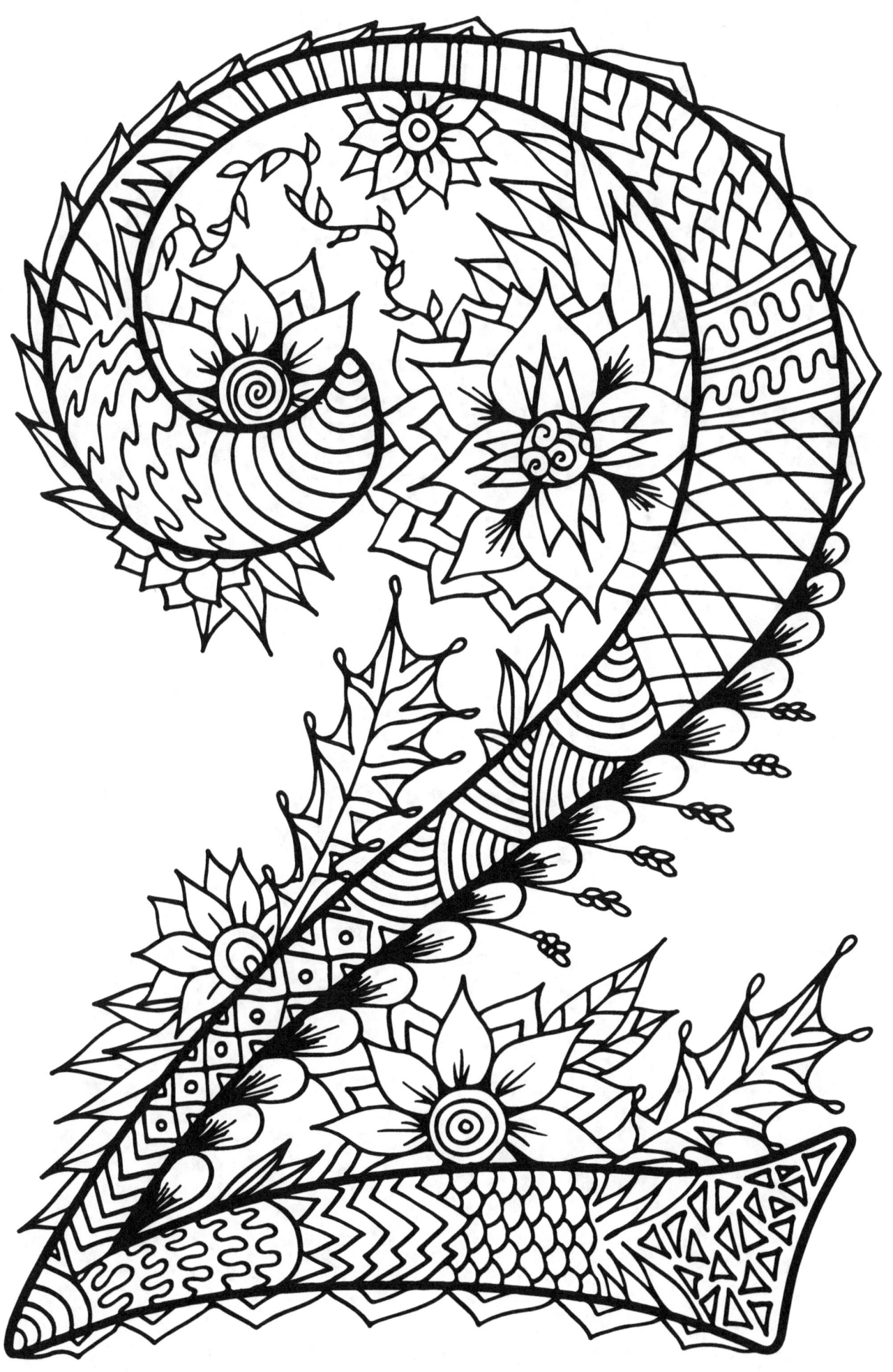

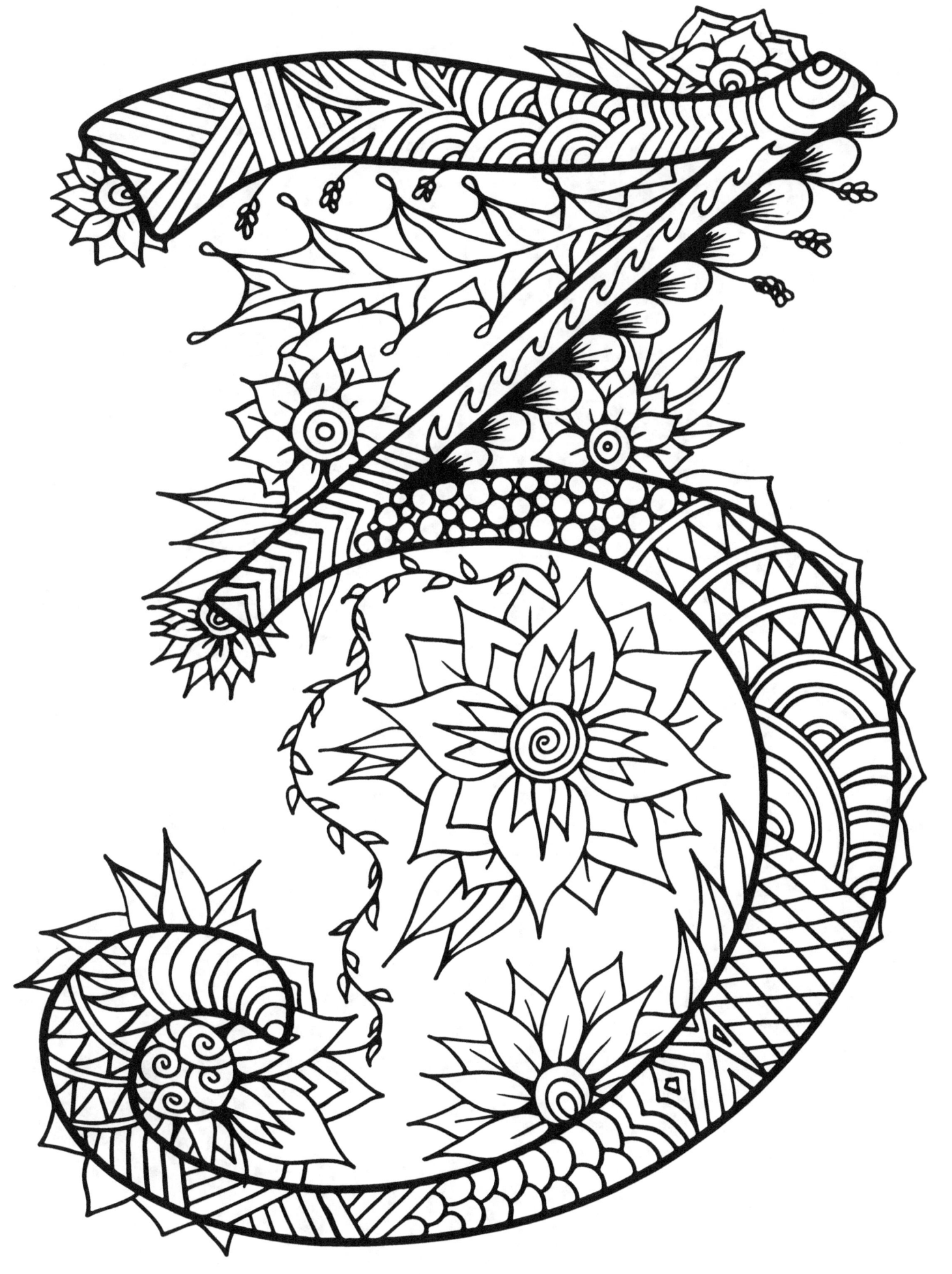

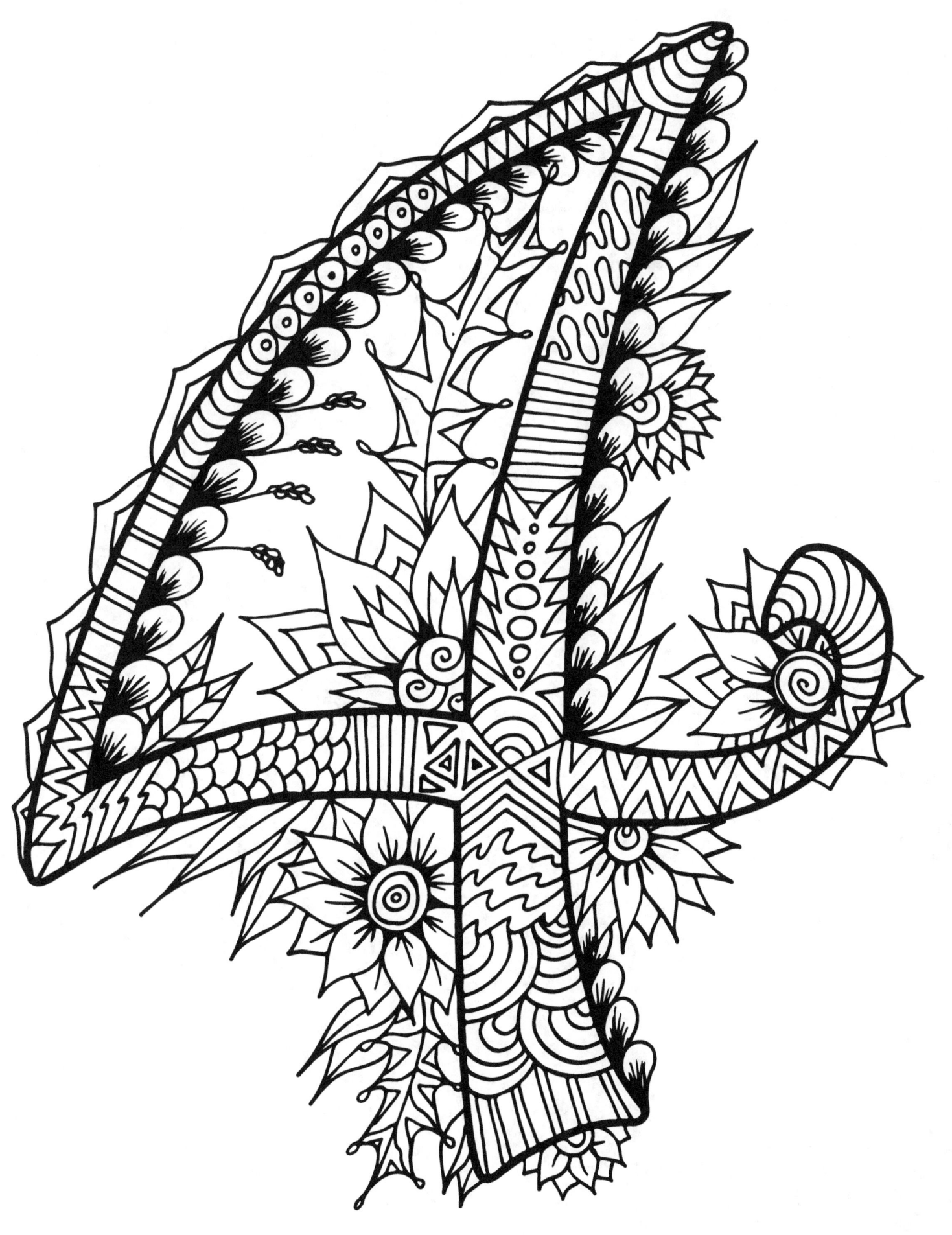

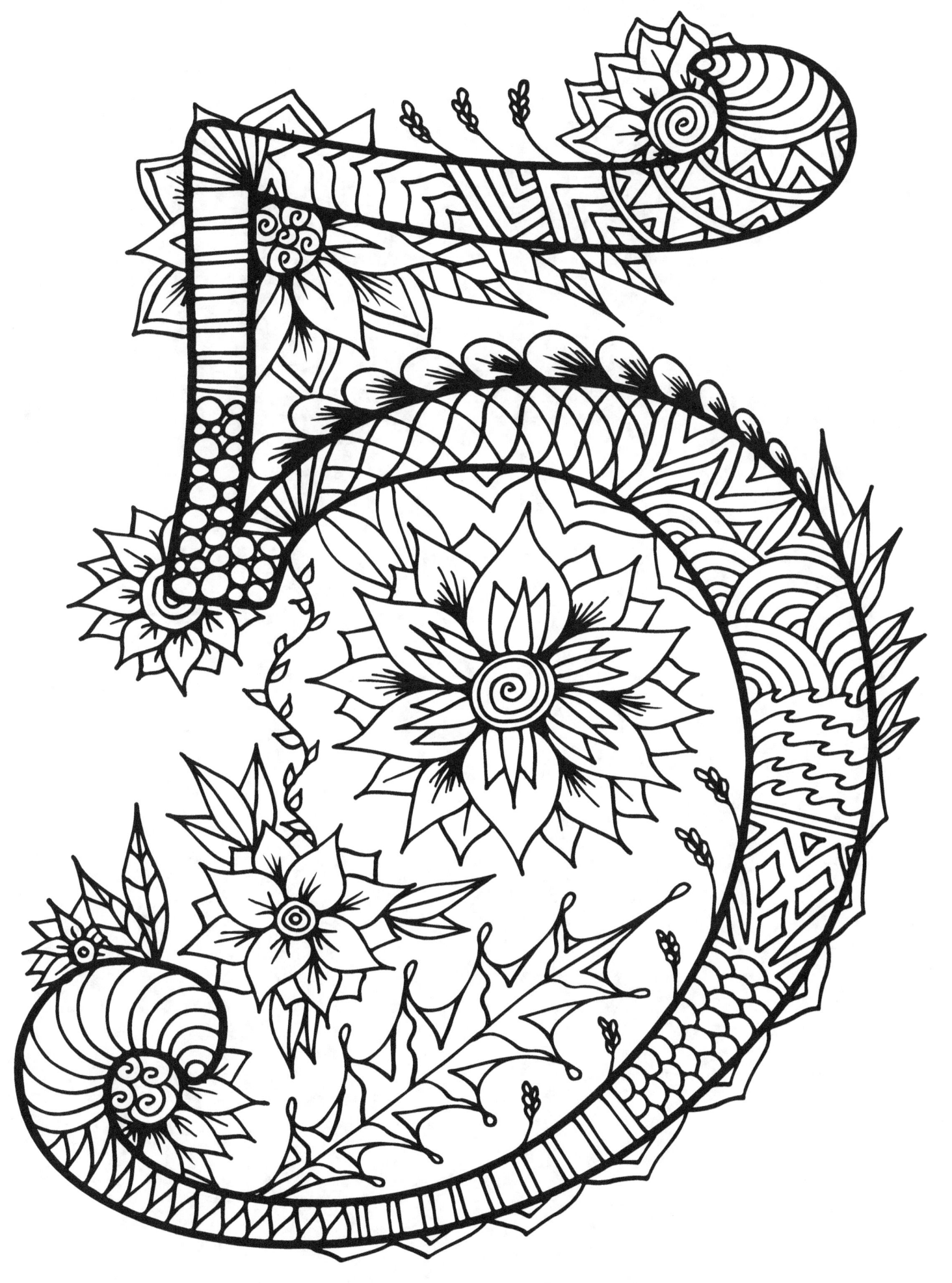

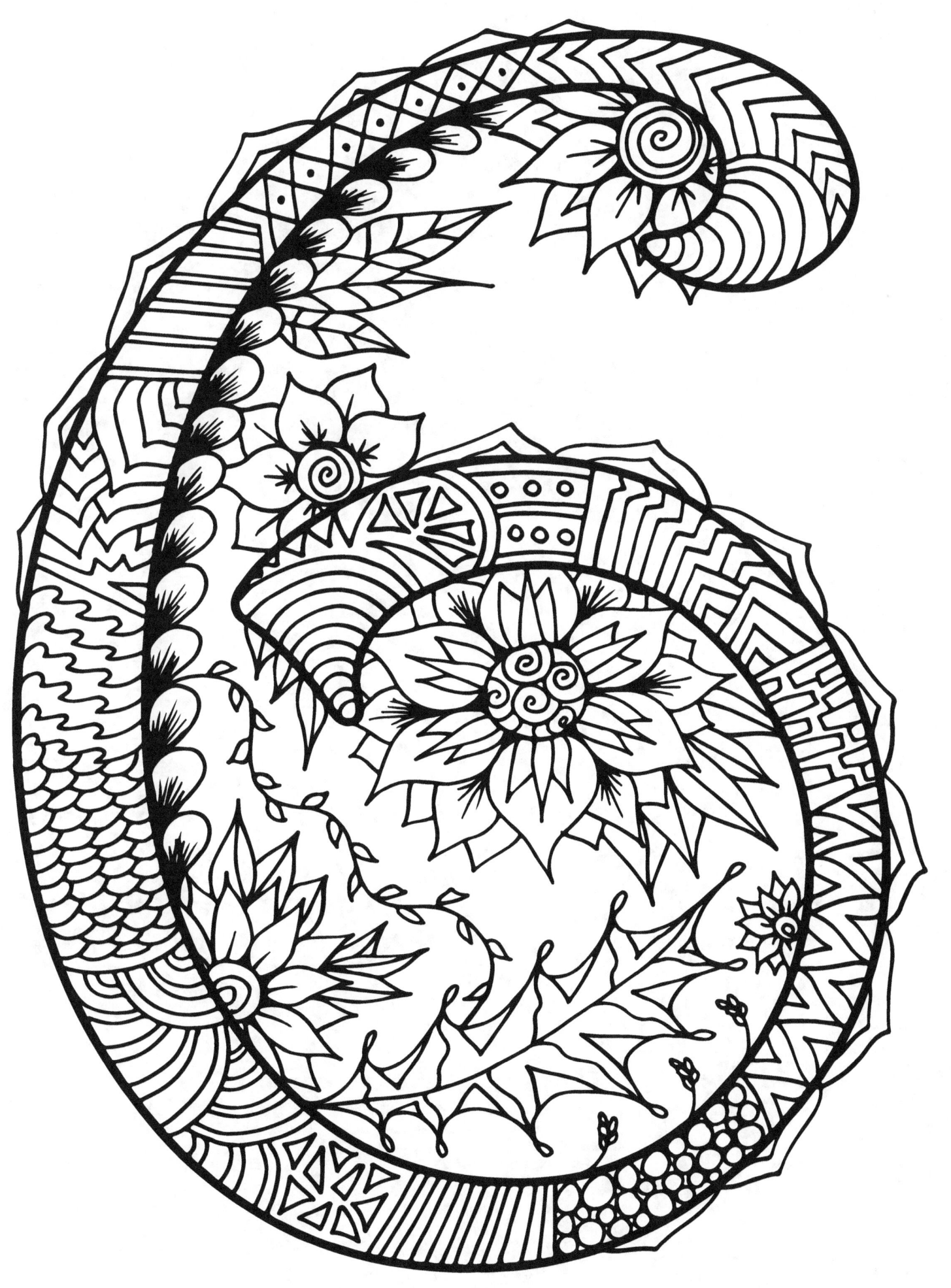

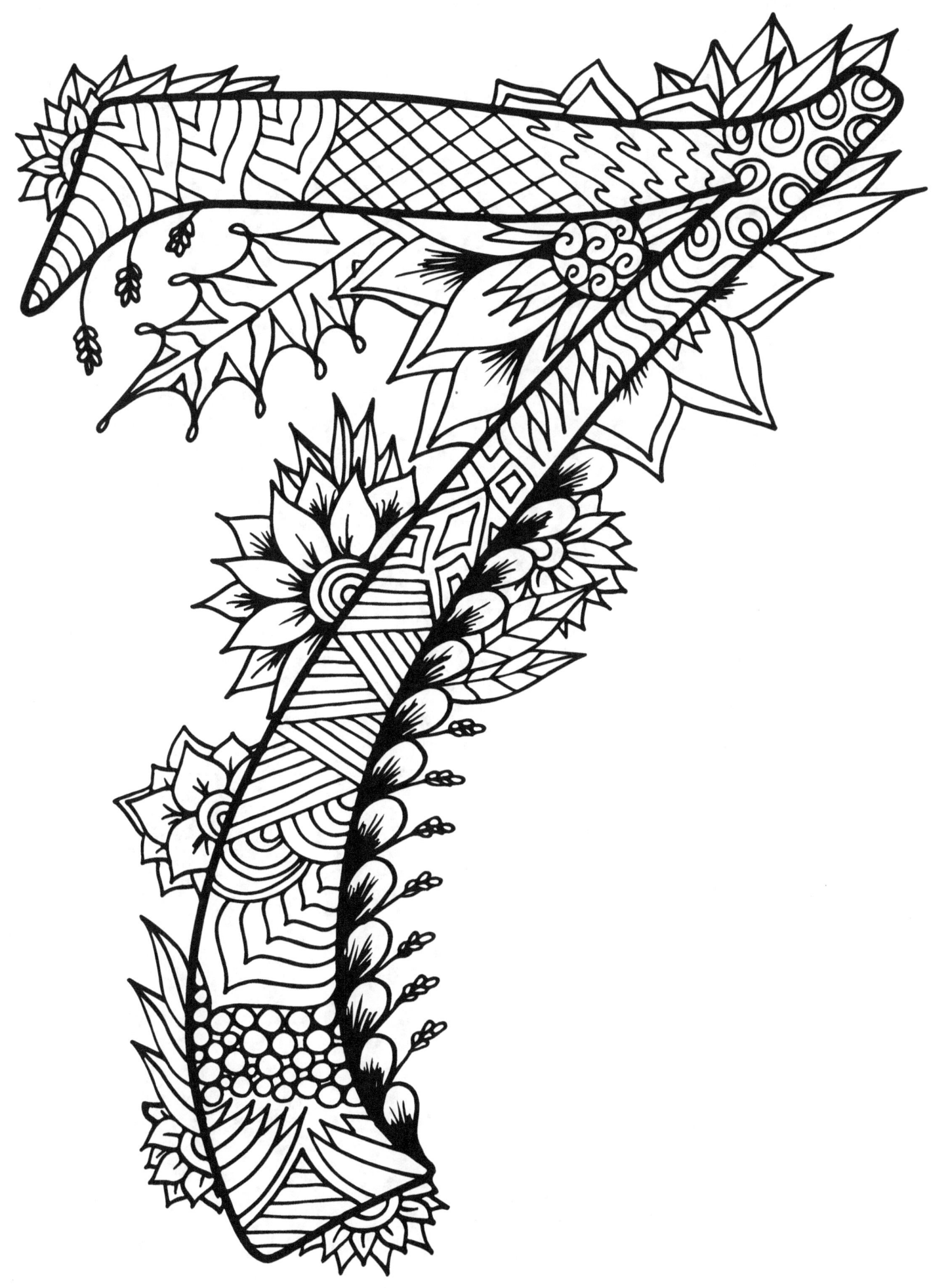

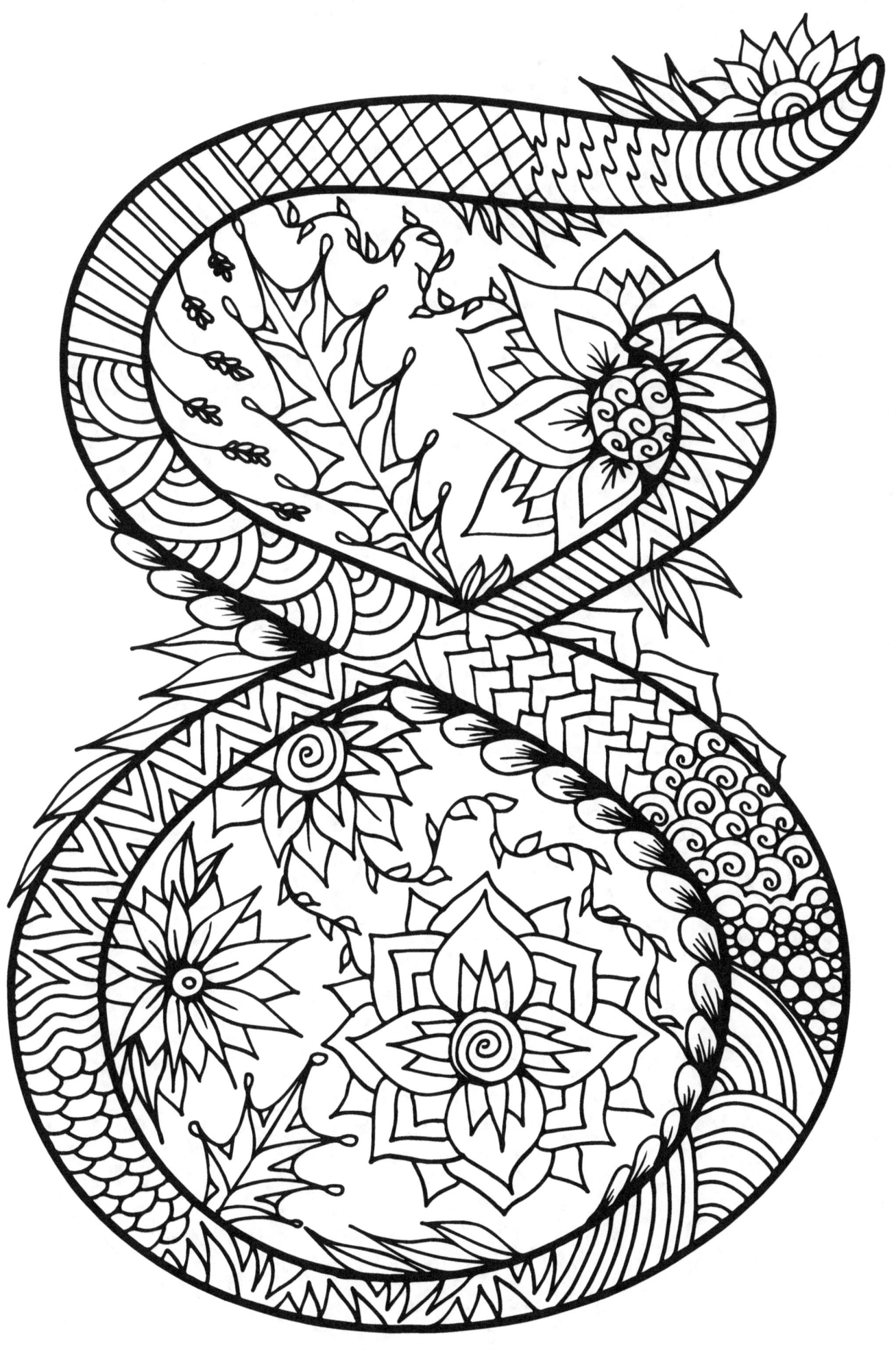

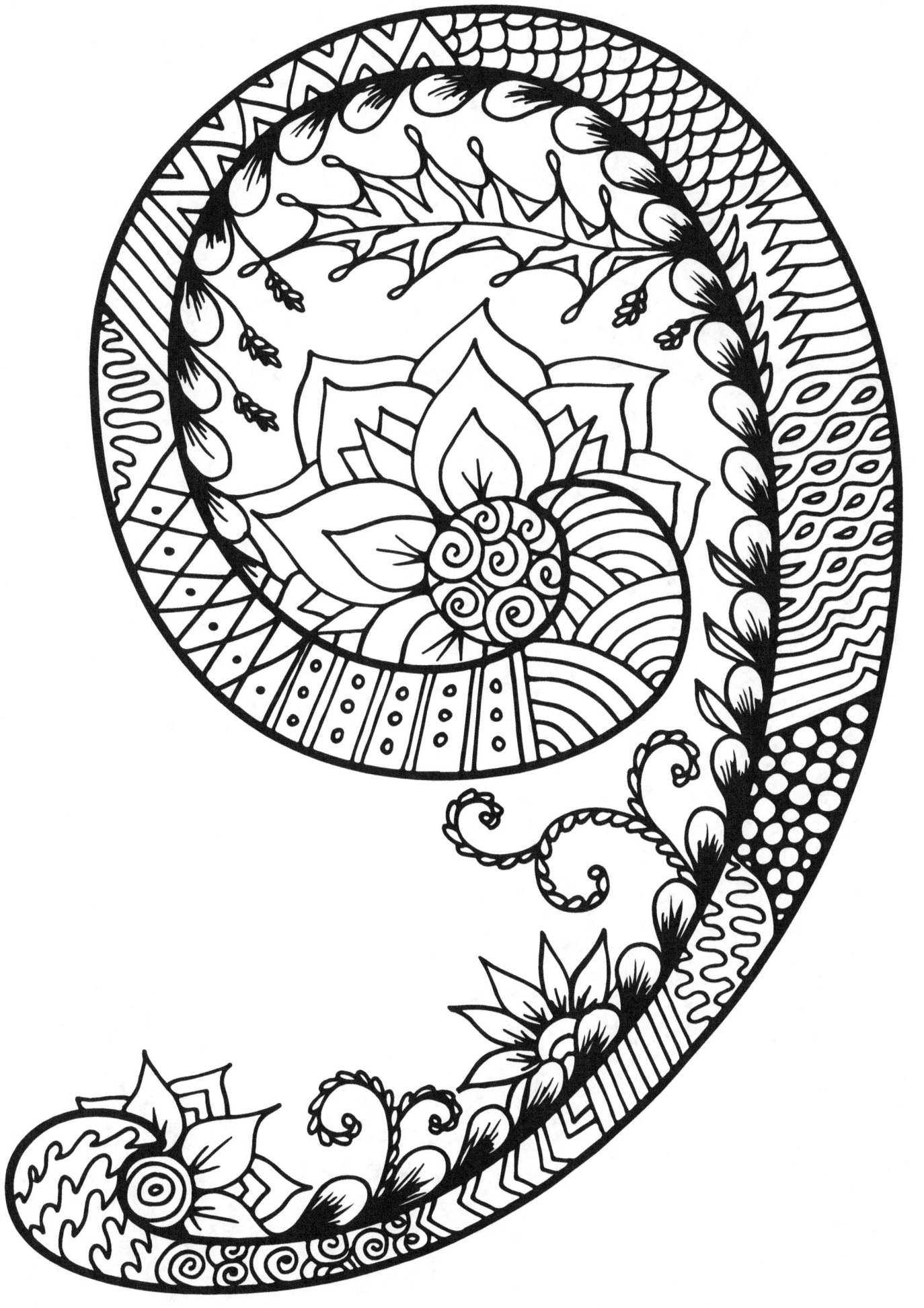

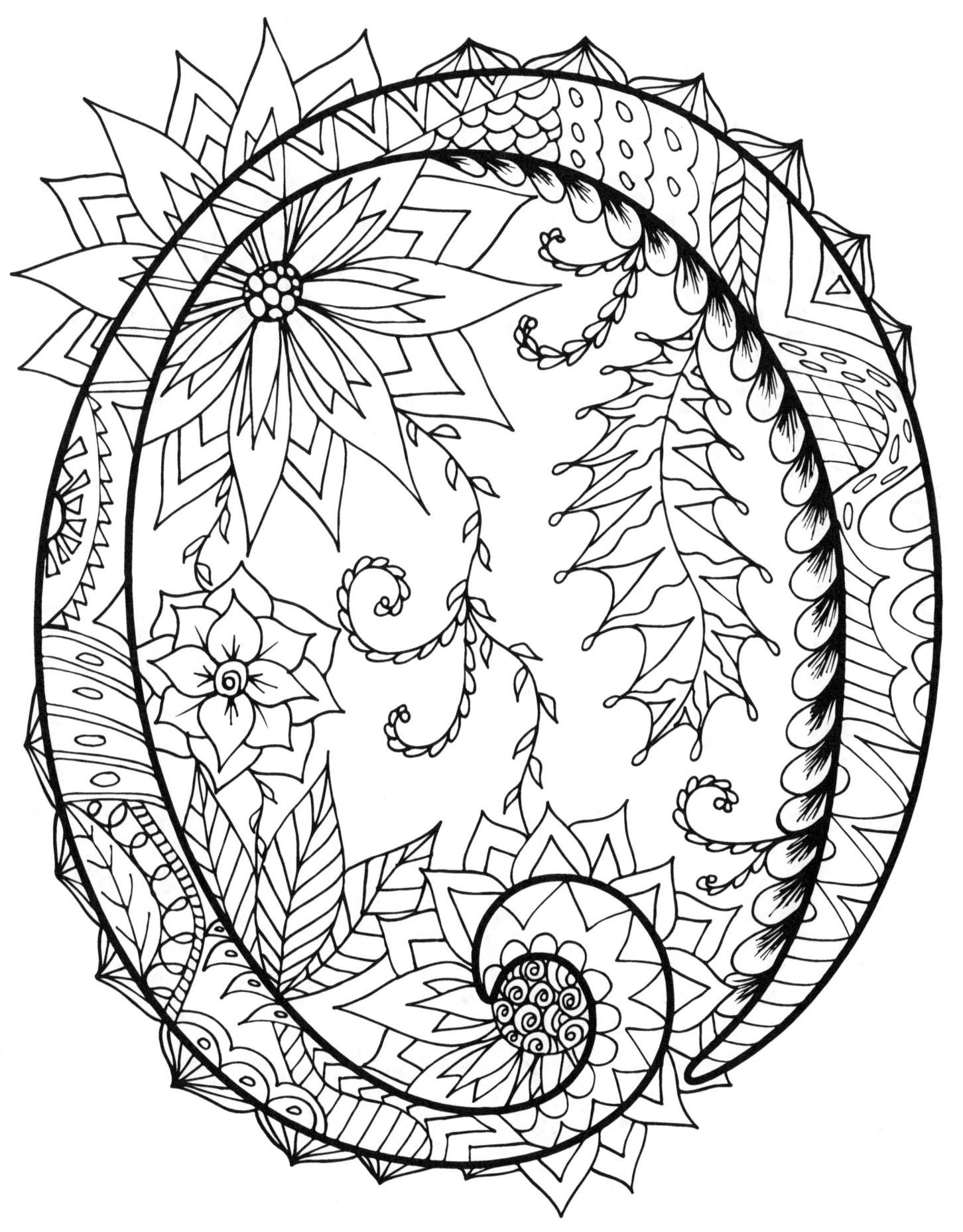

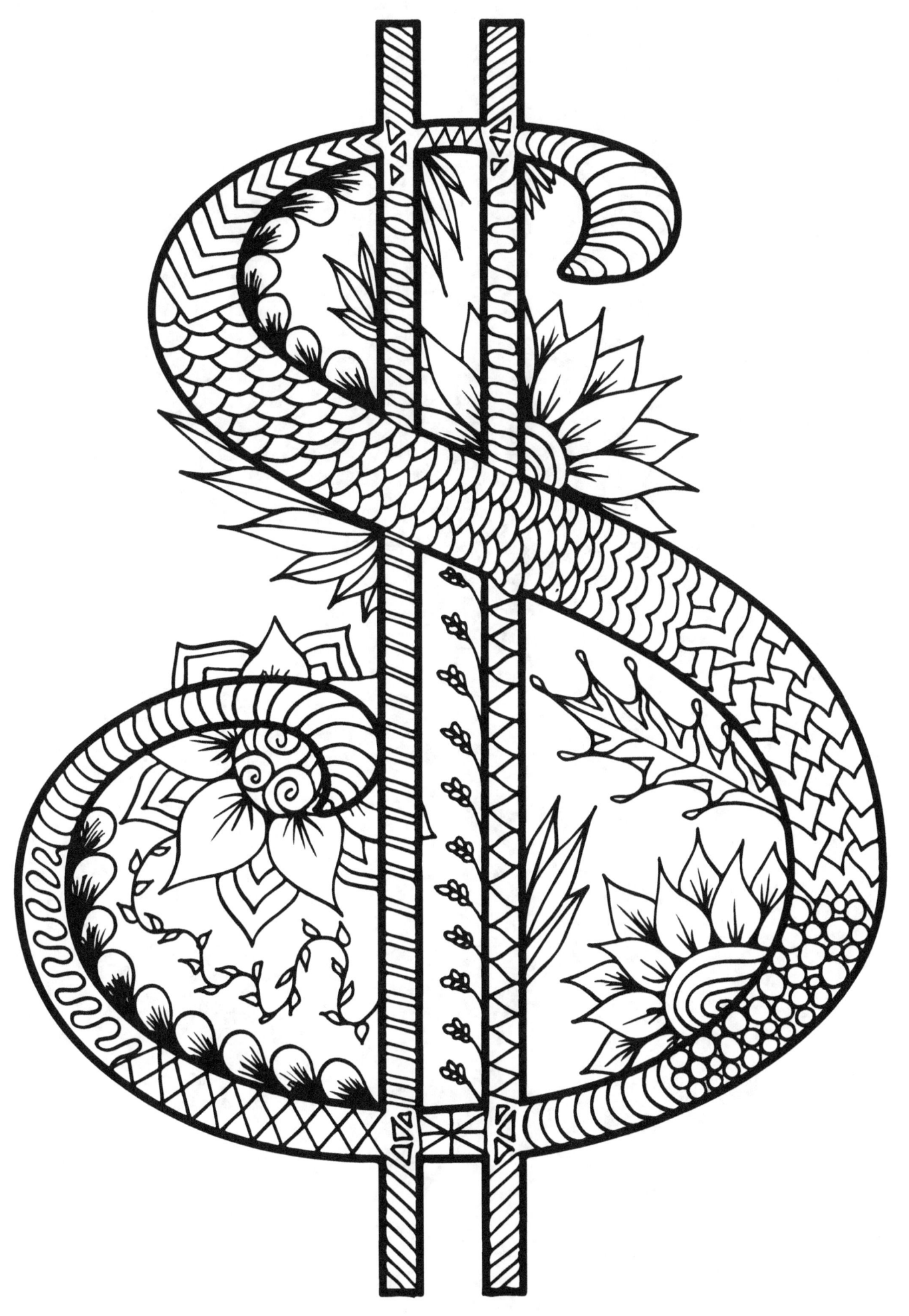

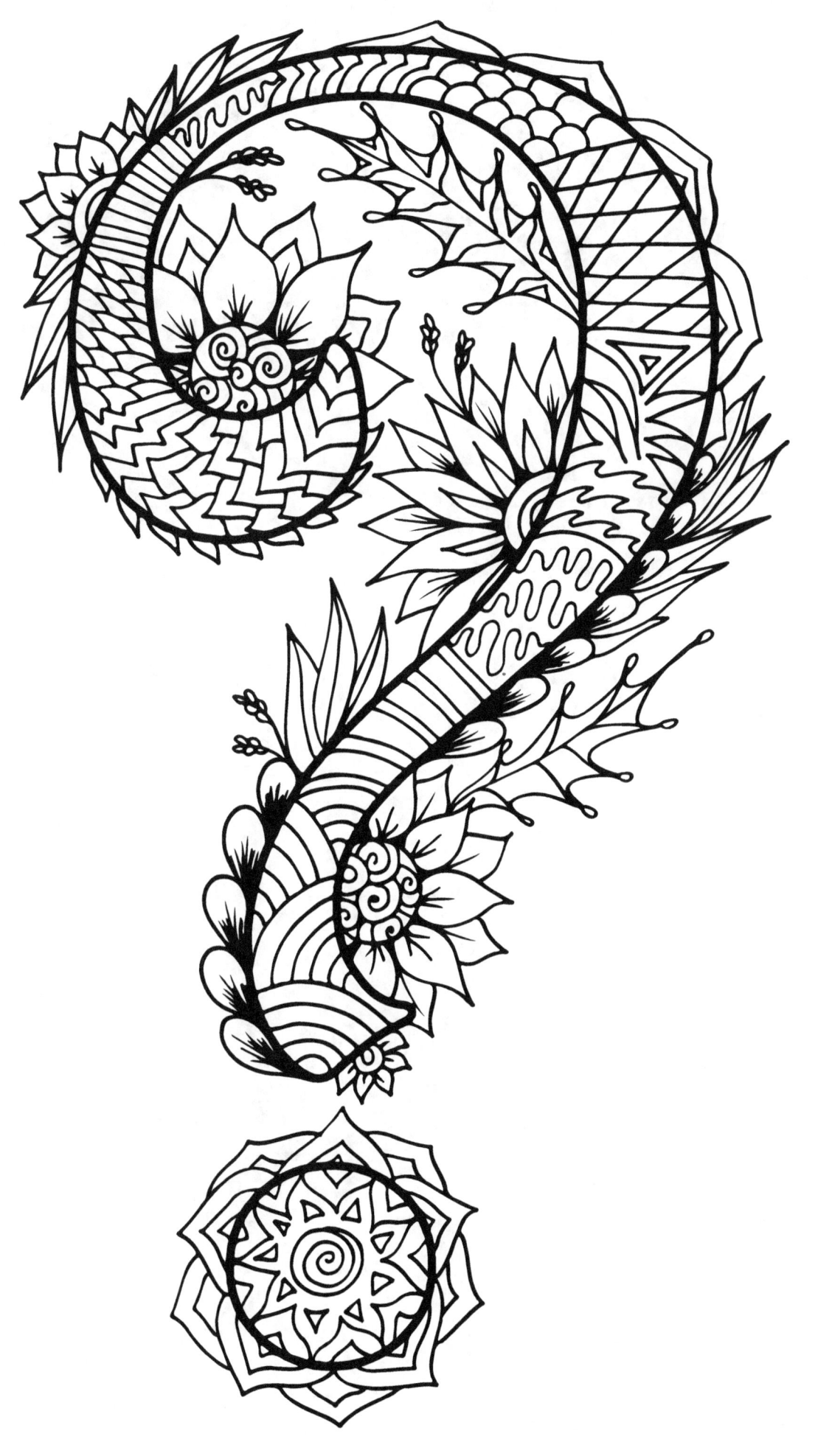

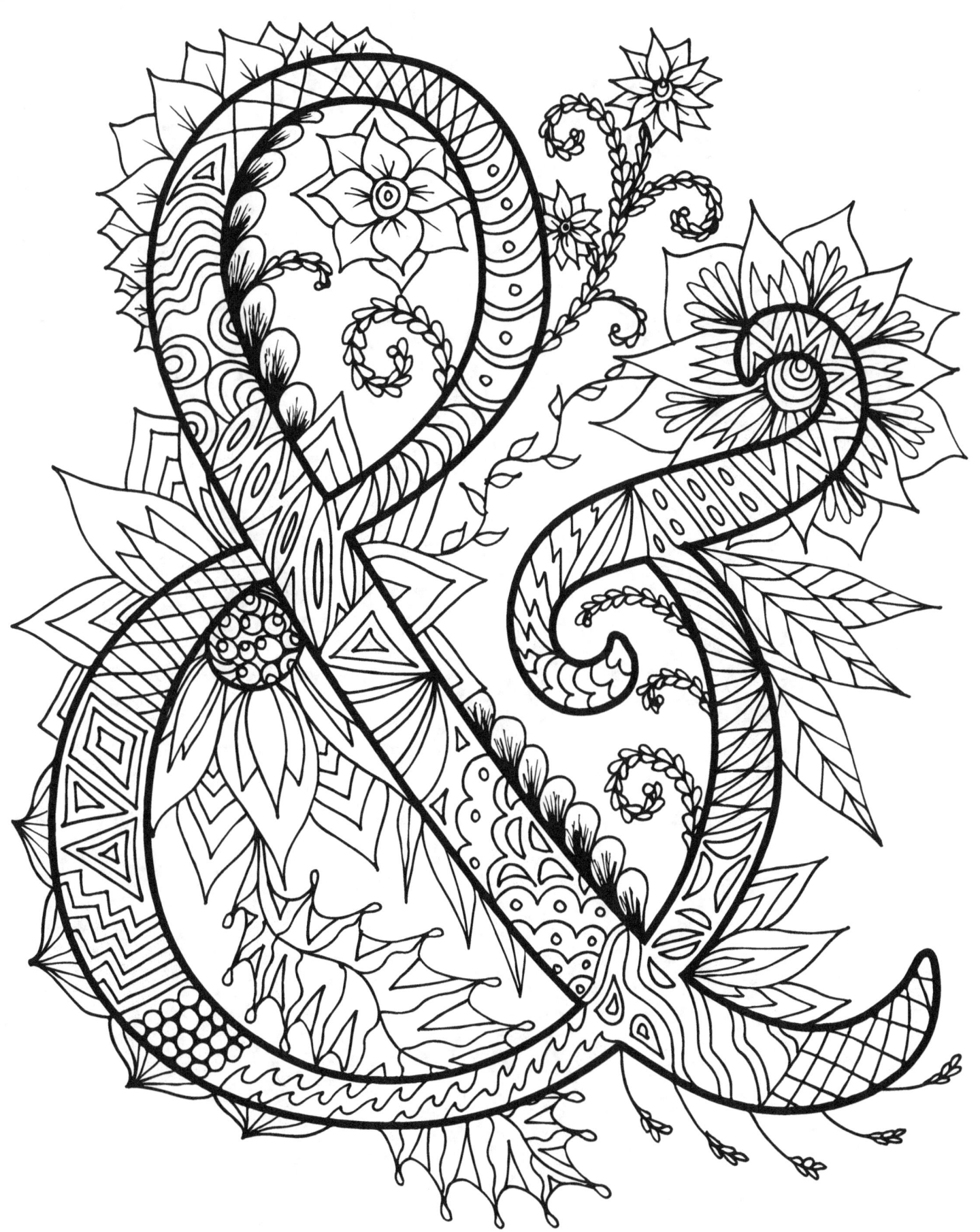

www.ingramcontent.com/pod-product-compliance
Lightning Source LLC
Chambersburg PA
CBHW080519220526
45465CB00006B/2537